BARBARA A. PERKINS, M.A., PCC | *Human Development*

COACHING YOURSELF ON JOY

A SPIRITUAL COACH'S PERSPECTIVE

Foreword by THEA MONYEE´
Licensed Marriage Family Therapist

KP PUBLISHING COMPANY

COACHING YOURSELF ON JOY

A SPIRITUAL COACH'S PERSPECTIVE

BARBARA A. PERKINS

KP PUBLISHING COMPANY

ISBN: 978-1-960001-88-7 (Paperback)
ISBN: 978-1-960001-89-4 (eBook)

Library of Congress Control Number: Pending

Cover Design & Photography: Addis Huyler
Literary Director: Sandra Slayton James

Published by:

KP Publishing Company
Publisher of Fiction, Nonfiction & Children's Books
Las Vegas, NV 89117
www.kp-pub.com
Printed in the United States of America

COACHING YOURSELF

ON

JOY

A JOYFUL DECLARATION

Coaching Yourself on Joy, is the culmination of a deeply spiritual, personal, and professional journey, presented as the final project and requirement for my Doctor of Ministry Certification. For 25 years, I have served as a life coach and spiritual practitioner, dedicating my life and work to helping Black women navigate life's complexities with resilience, faith, and a renewed sense of purpose. Through hundreds of workshops and one-on-one coaching sessions, I have witnessed firsthand the unique challenges Black women face and their incredible capacity for transformation when equipped with the right tools and spiritual guidance.

Coaching Yourself on Joy is the fourth book in my *Coaching Yourself* series, which includes previous works on marriage, betrayal, and grief. Each book in the series was born out of my commitment to providing practical, accessible, and spiritually grounded resources for women seeking healing and growth in these specific areas. However, this roadmap takes a distinctive approach by focusing on the spiritual principles that serve as the foundation for experiencing true, lasting Joy. Joy and Peace are the common searches that many struggle to find and sustain. In my practice, I have found that Joy is often conditional and transactional in the lives of many Black women whom I have served. I often hear and sense women's distress due to the lack of Joy in the way they hope for.

Joy, as I have come to understand it through my journey and the lives of the women and mentor-teachers I have had, is not a fleeting emotion tied to external circumstances. Rather, it is a state of being deeply rooted in our faith and relationship with God. This book is an invitation to embrace Joy as a choice, even during life's most painful disappointments, losses, and challenges. It is a guide to rediscovering the divine gift of Joy and allowing it to bring peace and purpose into our lives. Placing Joy in the center of our daily lives is an opportunity to live a life driven by a practice of care. Self-care as an essential part of living a life of Joy is on top of my list.

As I embark on this last step in this academic journey, *Coaching Yourself on Joy* represents the fulfillment of a scholarly and biblical requirement and a labor of love. It continues my life's work and reflects my unwavering belief that Joy is our birthright and a divine promise. I hope this work will serve as a beacon for readers, empowering them to reclaim their Joy and walk boldly in faith, love, and purpose.

DEDICATION

Dear Black Women,

Coaching Yourself on Joy is for you. To the women who have carried the world's weight on their shoulders with grace, resilience, and immeasurable strength. To the mothers, daughters, sisters, and friends who have nurtured communities, built nations, and led movements, often without recognition or rest. To the women whose brilliance, wisdom, and vision have shaped history and continue to guide the future.

You have been the backbone of our communities, our democracy, the architects of justice, and the heartbeat of progress. In the face of disparity and the trials of inequity, you have risen time and time again, undaunted, unyielding, and unstoppable. You have loved deeply, fought valiantly, and endured mightily, all while uplifting those around you.

But now, it is *our turn!*

This transformational guide is a celebration of you and a call to action to prioritize yourselves as you have prioritized others for generations.

It is a reminder that Joy is not a luxury, but your birthright given by God. You deserve the fullness of life, the sweetness of peace, and limitless Joy.

To the sisters I have stood beside in the trenches for over four decades, this is my shout-out: We see you. I see you. It is time for us to embrace Joy unapologetically, to claim it fiercely, and to live it abundantly.

With love, reverence, and in solidarity,

Barbara

DEDICATION

To: Joy Reid,

Fearless creator of The Reid Out, and to the enduring spirit of our ancestors. On February 24, 2025, as your groundbreaking Joy Reid Show on MSNBC came to an abrupt close, your luminous voice only grew stronger, a beacon of truth in a season of cruelty, political weaponization, and relentless lies by those in power.

You have long been a brilliant Truth-Teller, a courageous warrior whose words cut through deception and injustice.

I met you first as an extraordinary journalist and later through the mutual connection with your tribe member, LaTosha Brown. In moments when it might seem easier to run or hide, you remind us with steadfast conviction: "They don't know Us. They not like Us."

We stand with you, Joy, as you have stood for US. We will show, not tell, our collective power, and THEY will know.

This dedication is not only for you, Joy, but also for the ancestral spirits who have guided us for generations. Their wisdom, strength, and unyielding commitment to justice light our way as we march forward on the path to victory. May your indomitable spirit continue to inspire, uplift, and lead us into a future defined by truth, Joy, and liberation.

With deep respect, unbreakable solidarity, and boundless gratitude,

Barbara

FOREWORD

Years ago, while mid-grind, juggling marriage, a full-time job, a side hustle, three kids, and being the resident therapist for everyone in my life, I asked myself a revolutionary question that radically changed the trajectory of my life:

DOES THIS BRING ME JOY?

In the midst of all the accomplishing, surviving, navigating, and planning, we fail to ask questions that force us to evaluate how we exist. To take it a step further, we fail to see how we have been conditioned to think of many of the fruits of the Spirit, such as peace, love, and especially Joy, as luxuries we must earn through the struggles of life, as opposed to our righteous inheritance.

Coaching Yourself on Joy is here to remind us that all the fruits of the Spirit are available to us if we believe.

Being in the company of the incomparable Barbara A. Perkins can only be described as a JOYFEST! A fierce and powerful force for change, purpose-centered living, and empowerment wrapped in a glowing smile that beams warmth across any space, virtual and in-person. Her work and writings offer insight into how to keep and sustain our glow during times of uncertainty and in the face of adversity. In this work, *Coaching Yourself on Joy*, Perkins provides a roadmap to reclaim, sustain, and step boldly into our Joy without apologies.

Her Love is evident in the book's layout. The chapters are constructed to anticipate the reader's needs, inner thoughts, and even external roadblocks to creating a life that says, MY JOY MATTERS! Perkins' experience as a leader, spiritual coach, and mentor shines throughout this intentional and practical curriculum, making it a must-use guide for those who seek success, pursue purpose, and believe neither has to come at the expense of our Joy and wellbeing.

Before you turn to the next page, I want to invite you to pause, inhale, exhale, and create space in your mind and body to read the contents of this book and, more importantly, embody them. Allow the wisdom and practices shared here to become a part of you, a part of your journey, and above all, please enJOY!

Thea Monyeé,
Founder of The Joy Centered Living Experience

PRAISE BY
DR. RUBY LONG

Barbara A. Perkins expertly navigates the tumultuous waters of life, offering readers a transformative journey toward enduring Joy. As a seasoned healer, daughter, friend, and Joy seeker, I have witnessed the absence of Joy in the lives of those I care for. Barbara's insights provide a beacon of hope and practical wisdom, encouraging readers to find Joy in fleeting moments of happiness and as a resilient force during life's darkest times.

Coaching Yourself on Joy invites us to explore the countless moments where Joy can infuse our souls, acknowledging life's inherent imperfections. Barbara guides queens of all walks of life to embrace their birthright of Joy through profound reflections. Her words remind us that, despite life's tempests, the anchor of Joy within can stabilize us. This journey is shared; we are not alone, even in the roughest waves. Embracing Joy becomes a summoning of peace, transcending life's chaos.

Barbara's book is a testament to the belief that every individual deserves unconditional Joy each day. In gratitude for the restoration and Joy we all deserve.

CONTENTS

INTRODUCTION

"You make known to me the path of life; in your presence there is fullness of Joy; at your right hand are pleasures forevermore."

Psalm 16:11 (NIV)

For many of us, life can sometimes feel like an intricate balancing act, a delicate dance between the extraordinary expectations of both culture and society. For twenty-five years, I have had the privilege of serving as a Life Coach and an Executive Coach, primarily working with Black women, who often are shouldering the weight of these immense expectations. It is a burden that can make life seem unrewarding and sometimes overwhelming.

In my private practice, I have worked with high-profile and successful career women who consistently deliver on every expectation placed before them. I have seen firsthand Black women's incredible strength and resilience, and often reminded them of how much the world depends on their brilliance, strength, and resilience. All of this is without equal value or appreciation for their significant contributions.

Despite the demands and responsibilities and the hustle and bustle of life, it is easy to forget this vital thing: we all deserve Joy. Joy should not be a seasonal commodity that we should reserve for special occasions or fleeting moments of happiness. Joy is a choice, and it can become our way of life. Joy is a lifestyle available to all who seek it, and grab hold of it as a necessity.

Ten years ago, I began this quest and personal journey that led me to make Joy the default setting in my life, even when circumstances seemed less than favorable, and life aimed its inevitable curveballs directly at me. What you are about to read is a collection of essays and insights from that transformative journey. It is about intentionally choosing Joy when the world and circumstances suggest otherwise. These pages explore self-awareness and the commitment to becoming the best version of ourselves, who I believe we were created to be. At the core, this work is an acceptance of the promise of God found throughout the Bible, that if we trust him and lean on Him, Joy and so much more will be ours.

Through these pages, seven essays presented as chapters, I will make a compelling case for elevating Joy in life to help you uncover the wellspring of Joy that already resides within you. Consider this guide as a roadmap to finding Joy and making it a constant companion on your life's journey.

Together, we will explore the power of perspective and how it can transform your experiences. We will assess some of the challenges that come our way and discover how to rise above them with a heart full of

Joy. And, through personal anecdotes, shared wisdom, and experiences, we will forge a path towards a life where Joy is not a rare visitor but a cherished friend who walks beside us daily, and every step of the way.

This is your invitation to join me on a quest for Joy. Making Joy a way of life and affirming that having the fullness of Joy is not a simple wish; it is a birthright given by God and a wise choice we are blessed to make. Let us uncover together the Joy that awaits all and any who desire it. The source and supply are endless.

Coach Barbara

> *"May the God of hope fill you with all Joy and peace as you trust in him."*
>
> Romans 15:13 (NIV)

1

CHAPTER

*An Essay on the
Search for Joy*

1
SEARCH FOR JOY

"This is the day the Lord has made; let us rejoice and be glad in it."
Psalm 118:24 (NIV)

"The more you praise and celebrate your life, the more there is in life to celebrate."

—Oprah Winfrey

In our search for Joy, we begin a journey to understand its essence, distinguish it from happiness, and uncover where and how to find it. In this first chapter, let us explore the nature of Joy, discuss the difference between happiness and Joy, and discuss the path to a Joy-filled life.

WHAT IS JOY?
Joy is a profound and enduring sense of contentment, fulfillment, and well-being transcending fleeting emotions. It is a state of inner tranquility and deep satisfaction that radiates from the core of your being. Joy is not reliant on external circumstances or momentary

pleasures; instead, it is an intrinsic, soul-nourishing experience that remains steady despite adversity.

"The Joy of the Lord is your strength."

Nehemiah 8:10 (KJV)

This scripture reminds us that our strength is deeply connected to our faith's Joy and relationship with a higher power. I call that power source God. You may refer to that higher power as Jehovah, Allah, The Devine, The Great One, or the Creator,

When we find Joy in our faith, it becomes a wellspring of resilience in our lives.

While Joy and happiness are often used interchangeably, they are distinct experiences:

- Happiness is a transient emotion, a fleeting feeling of pleasure or satisfaction in response to external events or situations. It can be associated with achievements, possessions, or favorable circumstances. Happiness is like a sunbeam that warms your day but may disappear when clouds gather.

- Joy, on the other hand, is deeper and more enduring. It arises from within, independent of external factors. Joy persists even in the absence of happiness. It is the source of resilience that enables you to find beauty and meaning in life's most challenging moments, such as death, betrayal, or divorce.

"Though you have not seen him, you love him; and even though you do not see him now, you believe in him and are filled with an inexpressible and glorious Joy."

1 Peter 1:8 (NIV)

As human beings, the search for Joy is innate; it is an integral part of our existence. But where do we find it, and how do we uncover it, is one of the greatest questions.

Joy begins within. It is not something we acquire from outside sources but a treasure we discover within our hearts. To find Joy, we must first look inward, embracing our strengths, passions, and inner peace.

Gratitude is a pathway to Joy. When we appreciate life's blessings, big and small, we cultivate a mindset of inviting Joy. The act of counting our blessings amplifies our sense of contentment.

Joy often flourishes in our connections with others. Meaningful relationships, acts of kindness, and shared moments of love and laughter can be abundant sources of Joy.

Joy resides here and now. Joy is current. When we practice mindfulness and immerse ourselves fully in the present moment, we unlock the door to Joy. Every breath, every sensation, and every experience become an opportunity for Joy.

FAITH AND JOY

Faith and Joy are intricately connected. Faith provides a foundation for Joy to grow and flourish. When we trust in a higher power or have faith in the greater purpose of our lives, it brings a sense of peace and assurance that can lead to lasting Joy.

> *"May the God of hope fill you with all Joy and peace as you trust in him, so that you may overflow with hope by the power of the Holy Spirit."*
>
> Romans 15:13 (NIV)

A LIFE WITHOUT JOY

A life without Joy is like a barren desert, parched and without vitality. Without Joy, we become prisoners of our circumstances, victims of our negative thoughts, and trapped in a cycle of discontent. A life without Joy can lead to negative feelings when seeing Joy in the lives of others. The absence of Joy in our lives can negatively affect our well-being and overall quality of life. One potential consequence of a lack of Joy is emotional distress, which leads to feelings of sadness, depression, and emptiness. Prolonged emotional distress can affect mental health and contribute to conditions like clinical depression or anxiety disorders. Prolonged, Joyless lives are the catalyst for prolonged misery and discontentment.

A life without Joy can reduce resilience. Joy and positive emotions play a role in enhancing resilience. When Joy is absent, individuals may find coping with life's challenges and setbacks more challenging. Your ability to bounce back from situations that require mental strength and courage will be impacted.

A lack of Joy can strain personal relationships. It can make it difficult to connect with others emotionally, leading to strained relationships with family, friends, and loved ones. A Joy relationship assessment is extremely important, particularly as the relationship ages.

> "If you have only one smile, give it to the people you
> love. Don't be surly at home, then go out in the street
> and start grinning 'Good morning' at total strangers."
>   —Maya Angelou

When Joy is decreased, so is your motivation. Joy often serves as a motivating force, driving individuals to pursue their goals and aspirations. Without Joy, motivation can wane, leading to decreased productivity and a lack of enthusiasm for life's endeavors. Motivation is sometimes confused with discipline. In my experience as a Life Coach, I have observed some of the most disciplined women who lack motivation. The level of your Joy is connected to your motivation level. The absence of Joy can lead to the absence of motivation.

Joy is like medicine when it comes to your physical health. The absence of Joy can have consequences on our physical health. Chronic stress and negative emotions can contribute to a weakened immune system, increased inflammation, and a higher risk of various health problems. One of the first questions a physician will ask a patient is, "How do you feel?" Joy helps us feel better when there are diagnosed issues. My firsthand account of this is when I visited my oncologist for the first time. Towards the end of the extremely emotional visit, she said, "We are in this together, and you, Mrs. Perkins, have a special role to play. I will do all that I can to treat and eradicate cancer from your body. However, your attitude is just as important for the best outcome in this situation."

The lack of Joy can also lead to isolation: When people lack Joy, they may withdraw from social activities and isolate themselves. This isolation can further exacerbate feelings of loneliness and unhappiness. Isolation because of shame or embarrassment about the Joyless status of one's life will only make Joy even harder to maintain.

Loss of enjoyment is another indicator of the lack of Joy. People may find it challenging to enjoy life's simple pleasures and activities they once found pleasurable, such as hobbies, spending time with loved ones, or engaging in leisure activities. The lack of Joy robs us of the simple pleasures in our lives. These small and simple pleasures I call Joy elevators are important in our day-to-day engagements. So much so that I believe scheduling simple pleasures is a must do.

Life can seem extremely unfulfilling without Joy. An ongoing absence of Joy can lead to emptiness and unfulfillment in life, as individuals may feel like they are merely going through the motions without experiencing true happiness. When I hear clients speak of true happiness, it translates to Joy. The emphasized happiness most often describes a level of Joy the person seeks.

A consequence of the lack of Joy is the dependency on negative coping mechanisms. Some individuals may turn to unhealthy coping mechanisms, such as substance abuse or unhealthy eating habits, to fill the void left by the absence of Joy. A subtle and prolonged consequence can harm one's life in multiple ways.

A lack of Joy can prompt individuals to question their purpose and the meaning of life, leading to spiritual crises. If not addressed, this can become an area of great concern. The lack of Joy that leads to the questioning of one's very existence is troubling and dangerous. Suicidal rates have spiked in the past decade, particularly among young black people.

It is important to note that experiencing occasional periods of low Joy or happiness is a normal part of life, and everyone goes through challenging times. However, if the absence of Joy is persistent and negatively affects your life, seeking support from a mental health professional or counselor can be beneficial in addressing the underlying causes and finding ways to reintroduce Joy and positivity into your life.

The world can seem colorless in such a life, and even the brightest moments lose their luster. Depression, anxiety, and a pervasive sense of emptiness can take root, making it challenging to find meaning or purpose.

As we journey through this little book on coaching yourself, we will discover that Joy is not an elusive dream. Joy is a choice we make each day. We will explore practical strategies, stories of triumph, and the wisdom of those who have found Joy in remarkable circumstances. Together, we will uncover the path to a Joy-filled life where happiness is not fleeting but an enduring state of being. I aim to turn on or turn up your Joy meter and enlist you as a Joy carrier.

AFFIRMATION ON THE SEARCH FOR JOY

I embrace the journey of seeking Joy, knowing it is a path of
discovery and growth.

Every step I take, every choice I make, leads me closer to the Joy
that is meant for me.

I am open and curious, finding Joy in life's simple and
extraordinary moments.

The search for Joy teaches me patience, gratitude, and the beauty of
living in the present.

I trust Joy is always within my reach, waiting to be uncovered
and cherished.

Each day, I become more attuned to the people, places, and
experiences that bring me Joy.

I honor my journey, knowing that the search for Joy is as fulfilling as
the Joy itself.

I seek Joy, and my life is enriched by the treasures I find
along the way.

A PRAYER FOR THE SEARCH FOR JOY

Oh God,

Thank you for the endless supply of Joy available to us all. Thank you for being the source of Joy and telling us that it is ours if we choose to have it in our lives. Open our hearts and minds to this idea. I pray for every reader on this journey to have the courage and determination to search for the Joy you promised us all.

Joy is not a fleeting season of happiness but a deep, abiding assurance of Your Presence in our lives. Teach us to trust in Your promises and to draw closer to You, the ultimate source of our Joy. I join the community of believers who wish to promote Joy worldwide. I am writing this work as a tool that could be shared worldwide. It is my offer and service to You. I trust that these words reflect Your light, and I trust that they will inspire others to turn toward You in their search for Joy.

Father, I pray for every reader who will embark on this journey to discover Joy through the wisdom and love poured into these pages. May each page bring encouragement, each word offer hope, and each message lead them closer to the realization that Joy is not just a distant goal but a possibility in their lives. Let them find Joy in the natural beauty in the world, in the kindness of others, and most importantly, in the knowledge that You deeply love them.

Clear the path for those struggling to see Joy because there is so much hurt, pain, and suffering around them, dear God. I pray for them. For those who may be grieving or have suffered any major loss or disappointment, I pray for them as well. May Your comfort and peace meet them where they are. Remind them, Lord, that Joy is not the absence of challenges but the Presence of Your grace. Help them to choose Joy, even when it feels hard, and to trust that You are working all things out for their good.

Dear Lord, let these words be more than words on a page; let them be a vessel of transformation, an invitation to deeper faith, and a guide to a life filled with the radiant Joy that comes only from You. Joy Everlasting is what I pray for.

Amen.

Write your thoughts on the search for Joy

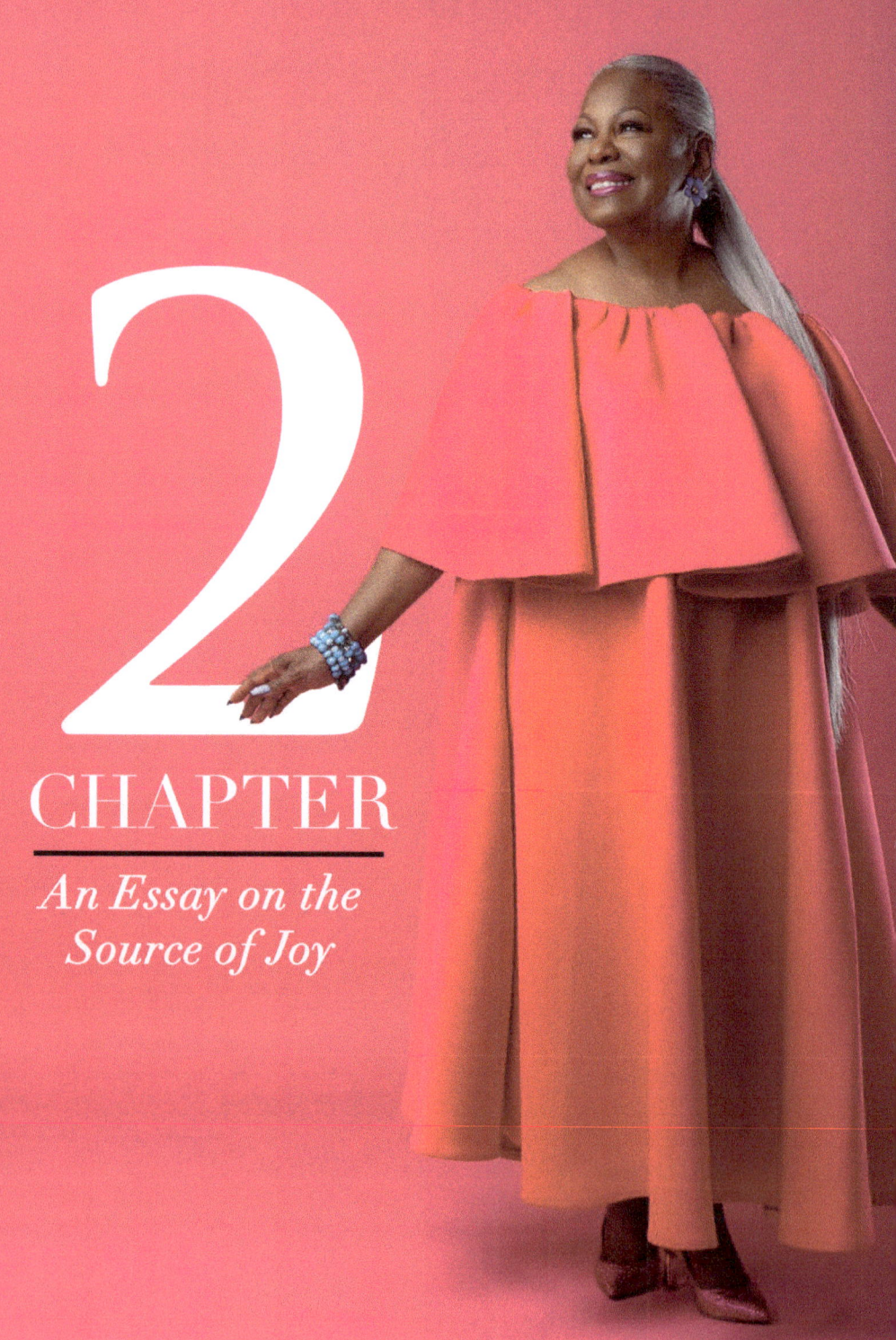

2

CHAPTER

*An Essay on the
Source of Joy*

2
SOURCE OF JOY

"Then will I go to the altar of God, to God, my Joy and my delight."

Psalm 43:4 (NIV)

"You are where you are today because you stand on somebody's shoulders. And wherever you are heading, you cannot get there by yourself. If you stand on the shoulders of others, you have a reciprocal responsibility to live your life so that others may stand on your shoulders."

—Cicely Tyson

Joy is an essential aspect of the human experience and is distinctively different from happiness. While happiness is associated with external circumstances or events, Joy is a more profound and lasting emotion that can be experienced even in adversity. The source of Joy can vary from person to person, but it typically arises from internal factors and deep-seated values.

Ultimately, Joy comes from within, driven by one's beliefs, mindset, values, and outlook. It is a state of mind that can be cultivated and nurtured through various life choices and practices. What have you chosen, and do you have a Joy practice?

Discovering Joy is like unlocking a treasure chest within your being. Here are tips on how you can begin your Joy journey:

1. **Cultivate Mindfulness:** Pay attention to the present moment with an open heart and an accepting mind. Practice meditation and mindful living to heighten your awareness of the Joy surrounding you.

2. **Practice Gratitude:** Keep a gratitude journal, regularly noting what you are thankful for. Gratitude shifts your focus toward the positive aspects of life.

3. **Simplify Your Life:** Declutter your physical and mental space. Simplifying your life can lead to greater clarity and allow space for Joy to flourish.

4. **Embrace Authenticity:** Be true to yourself. Authenticity brings a sense of inner harmony and Joy as you align your actions with your values and passions.

5. **Serve Others:** Acts of kindness and service to others can evoke profound Joy. Giving back and positively impacting someone's life is a sure way to find Joy.

6.   **Pursue Passion:** Engage in activities and hobbies that ignite your passion. Joy often accompanies pursuits that align with your interests and talents.

7.   **Seek Beauty:** Whether in nature, art, or everyday life, seek out moments of beauty and savor them. Beauty can uplift the spirit and infuse Joy into your day. Beauty is all around us.

8.   **Connect with Loved Ones:** Nurture your relationships with loved ones. Genuine connections and shared moments of laughter and love can be filled with Joy.

9.   **Practice Self-Compassion:** Treat yourself with kindness and self-compassion. Acknowledge your worthiness of Joy as you would affirm it for others.

10.   **Let Go of Control:** Release the need to control every aspect of your life. Embrace and accept the flow of being, understanding that not everything can be controlled, predicted, or curated to satisfy our view of how it should be.

This emotion called Joy is accessible to everyone who chooses it. The degree of Joy may vary from person to person and can be influenced by individual circumstances and mental health. Joy is a fundamental human emotion that people can experience in numerous ways and multiple seasons of life.

The question of whether we are born with Joy already inside of us, I believe, is a matter of philosophical and psychological debate. It is important to understand that Joy, as an emotion, is a complex interplay of biology, genetics, and individual experiences. There are a few different perspectives that I will share and break down for a deeper discussion. This is where you become your coach on the matter. Remember, I am your thinking partner and facilitator of the best answers you must uncover for yourself. Most of the work is up to you. The work is on the inside and you, and I are drilling down to where your best answers for yourself are.

1. **Biological Basis:** Some research suggests that there may be a biological basis for the capacity to experience Joy. Certain brain regions and neurotransmitters are associated with positive emotions, including Joy. These biological factors can be present from birth. However, the experience of Joy is influenced by a combination of genetic and environmental factors.

2. **Genetic Predisposition:** Genetics plays a role in determining an individual's baseline temperament or predisposition for experiencing Joy. Some people may have a genetic disposition that makes it easier to experience positive emotions.

3. **Environmental and Experiential Factors:** The experiences and environment an individual is exposed to throughout life significantly shape their emotional

responses. Early childhood experiences, family dynamics, and cultural influences contribute to an individual's capacity for Joy.

4. **Learned Behavior:** Joy is also influenced by learned behavior and cognitive processes. Over time, individuals can learn to focus on the positive aspects of life, practice gratitude, and develop a more Joyful outlook. This is where our faith has a profound influence on our Joy capacity.

"But the fruit of the Spirit is love, Joy, peace . . ."
Galatians 5:22 (KJV)

I believe that while biological and genetic factors may influence our capacity for Joy, it is also highly influenced by environmental, cultural, and personal experiences. It is not accurate to say that Joy is solely "inside" of us from birth. It is much more accurate to say that Joy is a complex intersection of nature and nurture, and individuals can actively cultivate and nurture their capacity for Joy throughout their lives through various practices and choices.

IS JOY SUSTAINABLE?

In a world where challenges and hardships are a part of life, it is natural to wonder if Joy can be sustained. The short answer is yes. Joy is not the absence of difficulties but the ability to find beauty, meaning, and moments of happiness even in times of adversity.

Sustaining Joy is about cultivating resilience and a mindset that embraces life's difficulties. It recognizes that while we may not control external events, we can choose how we respond. Rooted in faith and inner strength, Joy can remain constant, providing solace and hope even when the world seems bleak. The decision to be in Joy, to have a long-lasting relationship with Joy is to live life with an intention, a definitive purpose, and a promise to self. A way to address this idea of self-care beyond the "feel-good moments" curated often for external evidence.

THE MENTAL STATE OF JOY

Being in a mental state of Joy includes these five foundational habits to build upon until they become your daily practice:

1.   **Mindset Shift:** Cultivating a positive and hopeful outlook on life. Focusing on what is good and beautiful rather than dwelling on negativity.

2.   **Emotional Resilience:** Building emotional resilience to navigate challenges without losing sight of Joy. Acknowledging difficult emotions while also finding moments of happiness.

3.   **Presence and Mindfulness:** Engaging fully in the present moment and finding contentment in the here and now, regardless of surrounding circumstances.

4. **Faith and Belief:** Trusting in a higher power, a greater purpose, believing in a force much bigger, powerful than the human experience. Believing in the invisible master plan for good.

5. **Self-Compassion:** Treating yourself with the same kindness and love you offer others. Recognizing that you deserve Joy and happiness.

Joy is not a destination; it is a way of being. It is an ongoing practice that requires nurturing and cultivation. In each of these seven essays, we will look deeper into these principles, explore practical exercises, and share stories of individuals who have found Joy amidst life's challenges. Together, we will uncover the path to a sustainable and resilient state of Joy, even in a world where there is no shortage of trials, challenges, and tribulations.

In addition to being a writer and author of eight books, I am the Co-Founder, President, and CEO of the International Black Women's Public Policy Institute (IBWPPI), a humanitarian and philanthropic 501c3 nonprofit organization. Since 2009, IBWPPI has been involved with other organizations to provide disaster relief and support for women in seven countries, including Haiti, the Bahamas, West Africa, South Africa, Bermuda, Belize, the US, particularly in the rural south and most recently, as I complete the final chapters, Southern California-Los Angeles County Fires.

It has been a work of love to be in a community with Black women who are the architects for justice and warriors addressing disparities of all types in the United States of America. Our work and support of these communities have been more than inspirational. We have made a tremendous impact on systems of care and the well-being of these women, their families, and their communities. Their stories, although often difficult to hear at first, are now stories that I welcome because they all have a common theme of strength, resiliency, courage, and faith. Here are just a couple of examples:

Example 1: Women in Haiti—Rebuilding Amidst Adversity

Haiti, a nation often beset by natural disasters, has seen its people face unimaginable challenges. One such woman is Marie, a mother of three living in Port-au-Prince. In 2010, a devastating earthquake struck Haiti, leaving hundreds of thousands dead and countless others homeless. Marie's home was destroyed, and she lost family members in the tragedy.

Despite the overwhelming loss and adversity, Marie found solace and purpose in helping her community rebuild. She joined a local organization that provided shelter, food, and support to those in need. Through her work, Marie discovered that helping others brought her a deep sense of fulfillment and Joy. She realized that even during devastation, serving her community was a source of light and hope.

Example 2: Women in Abaco, Bahamas—Resilience After Hurricane Dorian

In September 2019, Hurricane Dorian, one of the most powerful Atlantic hurricanes on record, wreaked havoc in The Bahamas, particularly in

Abaco. It left entire communities in ruins, displacing countless families. Among those affected was Carla, a schoolteacher and mother.

Carla and her family lost their home, possessions, and their sense of security. Yet, in the aftermath of the disaster, she found strength and resilience within her tight-knit community. Carla made efforts to provide shelter, food, and emotional support to her fellow survivors. She witnessed the power of unity and the human spirit's capacity to endure and rebuild. Hope was never lost.

Example 3: Women in Pasadena—Altadena Fires, Los Angeles County

On January 7, 2025, while people were still exchanging New Year's greetings, wildfires erupted in Southern California. These fires raged for three weeks, resulting in the complete destruction of 18,000 homes across 57 acres of land and causing 29 fatalities. Tragically, this included a family member of a close friend who was found deceased with a garden hose in hand in front of his property.

Dianne, who also lost her home and all her possessions, partnered with IBWPPI to set up a monthly support center for 25 families who too lost everything they owned. Twenty-five families resulted in about 75 people.

Through these experiences, these brave women discovered a profound sense of purpose and an appreciation for the small moments of Joy that emerged as they too stood in these unimaginable circumstances. They recognized that even in the face of these horrific losses, community bonds and the determination to rebuild offered new glimpses of hope and happiness.

These stories illustrate the resilience and courage of women who have faced overwhelming adversities. They inspire examples of how, even in the most challenging circumstances, the human spirit can embrace Joy through acts of service, community, and the pursuit of purpose.

PHYSICAL WELLNESS PRACTICE

Physical well-being plays a significant role in supporting a Joyous state of mind. Here is an important list of physical conditions and practices that can contribute to and shore up your Joy reservoir.

Adequate Sleep: Getting sufficient, restful sleep is crucial for maintaining a positive mood and emotional well-being. Sleep allows the body and mind to rejuvenate, helping you approach each day with a brighter outlook. The older we get, the more sleep we need. Set a goal for daily sleep.

Regular Exercise: Physical activity releases endorphins, the body's natural mood lifters. Regular exercise can improve your mood, reduce stress, and increase happiness.

Healthy Eating: A balanced, nutritious diet of fruits, vegetables, and whole grains provides essential nutrients for brain health and emotional well-being. Proper nutrition can help stabilize mood and energy levels. Eliminate added sugar.

Hydration: Staying well-hydrated is essential for maintaining optimal cognitive function and supporting a positive mood. Dehydration can lead to feelings of fatigue and irritability.

Sunlight Exposure: Exposure to natural light, especially during the day, can positively impact mood. Sunlight helps regulate the body's internal clock and boosts the production of serotonin; a neurotransmitter associated with happiness.

Relaxation Techniques: Incorporating relaxation techniques such as deep breathing, meditation, or yoga can help reduce stress and anxiety, leading to a more Joyous state of mind.

Social Interaction: Engaging in social activities and maintaining healthy relationships can boost mood. The sense of connection and belonging is closely tied to happiness.

Pampering and Self-Care: Treating yourself to self-care activities like a warm bath, massage, or simply taking time for hobbies you enjoy can enhance your overall well-being.

Reduced Alcohol and Caffeine: Excessive consumption of alcohol or caffeine can negatively impact your mood. Moderation in these areas can contribute to a more balanced emotional state.

Physical Health Check-ups: Regular check-ups with healthcare professionals can help identify and address physical health issues affecting your emotional well-being.

Adequate Pain Management: If you have chronic pain or discomfort, addressing these issues through proper pain management can improve your mood and quality of life.

Regular Medical Check-ups: Regular medical check-ups help identify and address any underlying medical conditions that might affect your emotional health.

Regular Dental Check-up: Dental checks will help to keep any conditions that could lead to major problems in check. Dental issues are often overlooked.

Remember that everyone's physical and emotional needs are unique to them. What works for one person may not work for another. Therefore, listen to your body and mind and make choices that support you. I encourage seeking help from a healthcare professional who can provide specific advice and strategies for enhancing physical and emotional health. Make physical and emotional care an annual routine.

Creating a habit of expressing gratitude for the simple things in life can bring a sense of Joy. When you appreciate what you have, you experience Joy in the present moment. Even if you need to write down a gratitude statement and read it multiply times throughout your day. It will help you to establish a consistent habit of expressing gratefulness.

Connection: Meaningful relationships and human connections can be a major source of Joy. The love and support of friends and family can bring deep and lasting happiness.

Personal Growth: Achieving personal goals, pursuing passions, and growing as an individual is also a source of Joy. The sense of accomplishment and self-improvement can be deeply satisfying.

Acts of Kindness: Helping others and practicing acts of kindness generate a profound sense of Joy. Giving to others often leads to feelings of fulfillment. Giving can be as simple as a telephone call or a handwritten note of encouragement to someone else who may need that special consideration when you decide to do it.

Mindfulness and Presence: Being fully present in the moment, whether through meditation, mindfulness practices, or simply savoring the beauty of the world and all around you, can lead to a deep sense of Joy.

Creativity: Engaging in creative activities, such as art, music, writing, or any form of self-expression, is a source of Joy that allows you to tap into your inner passions and talents. Creating something new and creative can be exciting and Joyful.

Spirituality and Purpose: One out of two people I have asked says they find Joy and peace in having a spiritual practice and a sense of purpose. Belonging to a faith community and feeling connected to something greater can be uplifting and a source of Joy.

Resilience: Overcoming challenges and adversity has been the expectation of women. This is a major source of Joy. Bouncing back and growing from difficult experiences can be deeply rewarding.

"And those the Lord has rescued will return. They will enter Zion with singing; everlasting Joy will crown their heads. Gladness and Joy will overtake them, and sorrow and sighing will flee away."

Isaiah 35:10 (NIV)

AFFIRMATION ON THE SOURCE OF JOY

The source of my Joy is divine, eternal, and unshakable.
It flows from my deep connection with God, grounding me
in peace and love.

My Joy is not dependent on external circumstances; it is rooted in
the abundance within me.

I honor the source of my Joy by nurturing my spirit and embracing
gratitude daily.

This divine wellspring replenishes me, bringing clarity, strength, and
unwavering happiness.

Even in moments of challenge, I draw from this source, finding
comfort, resilience, and light.

The source of my Joy empowers me to live authentically, love
abundantly, and shine brightly. I celebrate this sacred gift, knowing
it sustains and guides me in all I do.

A PRAYER FOR THE SOURCE OF JOY

Dear God,

You are the source of our Joy. Thank you for the endless supply that fills us up each day. My cup runneth over, and I am grateful to give you all the praise.

Joy is your special gift to us, dear God, and it is free. Thank You for the gift of Joy, a light that shines within us, no matter the darkness all around us. Lord, help us to recognize that Joy is not dependent on circumstances but reflects Your unchanging presence in our lives.

Teach us to embrace our Joy, to claim it as a gift freely given by You. Let us stand firm in the decision to walk in Joy, no matter the challenges. Grant us the courage to let go of fear, guilt, and doubt so that our hearts may be filled with the peace that comes when there is Joy.

Guide us daily as we commit to practices that align with Your will. Help us always acknowledge our blessings when we stand on your word. Please help us always be grateful for the grace you extend to us, even when we do not deserve it. Thank you for the bodies we have that are healthy and the minds we have that are clear.

Remember that we deserve Joy because You have declared us worthy through Your love and mercy. Allow Your spirit within us to be the wellspring of our Joy, giving us inspiration, hope, and peace. Let our lives be a testimony of Your goodness and a reflection of the Joy that comes from knowing You and being in a relationship with You.

This is my prayer.

Amen.

What is your source of Joy?

Source of Joy

Source of Joy

3

CHAPTER

*An Essay on
Manifesting Your Joy*

3
MANIFESTING YOUR JOY

"Therefore, I tell you, whatever you ask for in prayer, believe that you have received it, and it will be yours."

Mark 11:24 (NIV)

"I need to see my own beauty and continue to be reminded that I am enough, worthy of love without effort."

—Tracee Ellis Ross

Joy is not merely a fleeting feeling or an outcome of favorable circumstances, it is a state of being that can be intentionally manifested through faith. As believers, we are called to live by faith, not sight (2 Corinthians 5:7). This principle extends to Joy. Through faith, we can manifest Joy as an active and intentional part of our lives, regardless of what is happening around us.

To manifest something means bringing it into reality and calling it forth through belief, intention, and action. As a fruit of the Spirit (Galatians 5:22-23), Joy is already present within us as believers. Yet, it requires our active participation in faith to bring it to the forefront of our lives. The Word of God gives us the blueprint for manifesting Joy, making it an occasional experience and a sustainable way of being.

THE ROLE OF FAITH IN MANIFESTING JOY

Faith is the foundation of manifesting Joy. Hebrews 11:1 (KJV) defines faith as

> *"Now faith is the substance of things hoped for, the evidence of things not seen."*

Joy, too, is often something we hope for, especially in difficult seasons. Faith allows us to claim Joy as ours, even before we feel it or see evidence in our circumstances.

Consider the words of Jesus in John 15:11(NIV),

> *"I have told you this so that my Joy may be in you and that your Joy may be complete."*

This promise reveals that Joy is not something we manufacture on our own; it is a gift from Jesus, made complete through our connection to Him. Our role is to believe in this promise and act in alignment with it.

When we operate in faith, we align ourselves with God's truth. We begin to see Joy not as a reward for good times but as a divine gift that can be accessed in all seasons of life. Faith shifts our perspective, allowing us to focus on God's goodness and promises rather than our challenges.

DESIGNING A LIFE OF JOY

Manifesting Joy is not a passive process, it requires intentional design. Romans 12:2 instructs us to *"be transformed by renewing your mind."* This renewal involves aligning our thoughts and beliefs with God's Word, which is full of assurances about Joy:

> *"The Joy of the Lord is your strength."*
>
> Nehemiah 8:10 (NIV)

Strength comes from Joy, and Joy comes from the Lord. When we choose to manifest Joy, we tap into a supernatural strength that sustains us through life's challenges.

> *"Rejoice in the Lord always. I will say it again: Rejoice!"*
>
> Philippians 4:4 (NIV)

Rejoicing is not just an emotional response; it is a spiritual discipline. It is a decision to focus on God's goodness and faithfulness, regardless of circumstances.

> *"You make known to me the path of life; you will fill me with Joy in your presence."*
>
> Psalm 16:11 (NIV)

Joy is found in God's presence. Designing a life of Joy means prioritizing time with Him through prayer, worship, and studying His Word.

To design a life of Joy, start by examining your beliefs. Do you believe Joy is available to you? Do you trust that God desires you to live in Joy? Your beliefs shape your actions, and your actions determine the reality you manifest.

PRACTICAL STEPS TO MANIFEST JOY

1. **Declare Joy Over Your Life**

   Speak Joy into existence. Proverbs 18:21 reminds us that "the tongue has the power of life and death." Use your words to affirm God's promises of Joy, declaring them over your life daily.

2. **Shift Your Focus**

   Manifesting Joy requires focusing on what is good, pure, and praiseworthy (Philippians 4:8). When negative thoughts arise, replace them with scriptures that remind you of God's goodness.

3. **Act in Faith**

   "Faith without works is dead." (James 2:26) If you believe in Joy, let your actions reflect that belief. Smile, give thanks, serve others, and engage in activities that bring you closer to God and His purpose for your life.

4. **Celebrate Small Wins**

   Joy is not always tied to big events. Celebrate the small moments of beauty and grace in your day. Gratitude is a powerful way to manifest Joy.

5. **Guard Your Heart**

   Proverbs 4:23 advises us to *"guard your heart, for everything you do flows from it."* Protect your Joy by avoiding environments, people, or habits that drain your spirit. Surround yourself with what uplifts and inspires you.

BIBLICAL EXAMPLES OF MANIFESTING JOY

The Bible is filled with stories of individuals who manifested Joy through faith:

- **Paul and Silas (Acts 16:25-26)**
  Even while imprisoned, Paul and Silas chose to sing hymns and pray. Their faith and focus on God manifested Joy, which led to a miraculous breakthrough.

- **Hannah (1 Samuel 2:1-10)**
  After years of barrenness and despair, Hannah prayed in faith and later rejoiced, praising God for His faithfulness. Her Joy was a direct result of her belief in God's promises.

- **David (Psalm 30:11-12)**
  David declared, "You turned my wailing into dancing; you

removed my sackcloth and clothed me with Joy." His psalms reflect a life of manifesting Joy through trust in God, even in times of great trial.

CONCLUSION: JOY IS YOURS TO MANIFEST

Manifesting Joy is an act of faith and intention. It is a declaration that you believe in God's promises, a commitment to design your life in alignment with His truth, and a decision to focus on the Joy already within you.

God has equipped you with the tools to manifest Joy. His Word, His Spirit, and His presence are your resources. You will find that Joy is attainable and sustainable as you align your faith with His promises.

Let Joy be the evidence of your faith, a reflection of God's goodness, and a gift you share with the world. Manifest your Joy, and let it transform your life into a testimony of His grace and love.

> *"May the God of hope fill you with all Joy and peace as you trust in Him, so that you may overflow with hope by the power of the Holy Spirit."*
>
> Romans 15:13 (NIV)

Joy is already within you. believe it, design it, and manifest it.

AFFIRMATION ON MANIFESTING JOY

I am a creator of Joy, and I manifest it in my life. Joy is my
natural state, and I attract experiences that amplify
my happiness and peace.

I align my thoughts, words, and actions with the energy
of Joy, opening the path for it to flow freely to me. I focus on
gratitude, abundance, and love, knowing these seeds grow into
moments of pure Joy.

I visualize a life filled with Joy, and the universe responds with
limitless opportunities to make it real. I trust in divine timing and
embrace the Joy that perfectly aligns with my highest good.

Joy radiates from me, surrounding my world with beauty,
positivity, and light.

Every day, in every way, I manifest Joy, which is mine to
cherish and celebrate.

A PRAYER FOR MANIFESTING JOY

Dear Heavenly Father,

Thank You for being the source of all Joy, the anchor of my peace, and the light that guides my path. I come before You with a heart open to receive the fullness of Joy you promised.

Lord, I ask that You fill my spirit with gratitude and wonder for the blessings You have already provided. Please help me to see the beauty in every moment and to find Joy in both the simple and extraordinary aspects of life.

Teach me, Lord, to release anything that weighs me down, such as fear, doubt, negativity, or pain, and to trust in Your perfect plan for my life. Open my heart to abundance, my mind to positivity, and my soul to Your divine Presence.

I pray for the strength to manifest Joy in every area of my life. May my thoughts align with Your goodness, my words encourage others, and my actions reflect the love and grace You have shown me.

Father, help me be a beacon of Joy for others, spreading light and kindness wherever I go. Let the pleasure I manifest inspire hope and healing in those around me.

Thank You, Lord, for the gift of Joy from knowing You and walking in Your purpose. I trust that You are always working for my good and that Your Joy will be my strength.

In Jesus' name, I pray.

Amen.

Write how you will manifest Joy.

4

CHAPTER

*An Essay on
Owning Your Joy*

4

OWNING YOUR JOY

"A happy heart makes the face cheerful, but heart aches crush the spirit."

Proverbs 15:13 (NIV)

"Hold fast to dreams, for if dreams die, life is a broken-winged bird that cannot fly."

—Langston Hughes

Joy is a universal emotion common in the range of emotions experienced by individuals and groups from diverse cultures and backgrounds. The internal motivation of Joy becomes rooted when we decide to own our Joy. When we truly have Joy and stand firm on our decision about being in Joy, our lives transform beautifully. It is a state of being that causes us to radiate positivity, contentment, and a deep sense of fulfillment.

Cultivating Joy is easier for some who are set on incorporating the practices discussed in chapter two, such as mindfulness, gratitude, and self-care. Engaging in activities and cultivating a mindset that aligns with your values and sources of Joy can help increase the presence of Joy in your life. It is your choice to make. Joy is ours to own when we believe we deserve it.

INNER PEACE AND ITS RELATIONSHIP TO JOY

Inner peace is the fertile ground where Joy takes root and flourishes. The stillness within allows us to rest in God's grace and mercy, even while life's uncertainties and storms seem unrelenting. The Bible repeatedly reminds us that God's grace is sufficient, and His mercies are new every morning (2 Corinthians 12:9, Lamentations 3:22-23). These gifts are not just assurances of His love but pathways to experiencing a profound, lasting peace that surpasses understanding (Philippians 4:7).

When we embrace the truth of God's unending grace that we are forgiven, loved, and held in His hands, we are freed from guilt, shame, and fear. His mercy, extended to us without limit, invites us to release regret and trust in His divine plan. In this spiritual state of peace, we create space for Joy to enter and dwell in our hearts. Our actions follow our hearts; therefore, our lives are examples of our beliefs.

Joy and inner peace are interconnected because Joy is often born from the confidence and security that come from knowing God is in control. When our souls are anchored in His promises, we are no longer swayed by temporary struggles or fleeting emotions. Instead, we experience a steadfast Joy, not because of our circumstances but because of the One who sustains us.

To live in Joy is to live in the awareness of God's peace, grace, and mercy, a reminder that no matter what we face, His love is greater. Inner peace is not the absence of challenges but the presence of God within us, calming the chaos and inviting us into the Joy of His everlasting care.

The mind requires peace to welcome and embrace Joy as a birthright. When calm and serene, the mind supports your travel through tough times. The mind, Joy, and faith are intricately woven together in the tapestry of a believer's life. The Bible teaches us to renew our minds daily (Romans 12:2) and to fix our thoughts on what is true, noble, and praiseworthy (Philippians 4:8). This mental discipline aligns our thinking with God's promises, cultivating a mindset of hope and trust.

Faith acts as the bridge between our minds and the Joy we seek. When we walk by faith and not sight (2 Corinthians 5:7), we trust God's sovereignty even when circumstances seem uncertain. This trust produces a Joy that is not dependent on external conditions but flows from the assurance of God's presence and provision.

Joy is the fruit of a mind centered on faith. When our thoughts are anchored in God's Word and faithfulness, our hearts overflow with a Joy that transcends understanding. Proverbs 23:7 (KJV) reminds us,

"As a man thinks in his heart, so is he."

A mind steadfast in faith creates a life infused with the unshakable Joy of the Lord, illuminating every step of the journey.

This is not to say difficult life moments will escape us. That is also not true. We will all be served massive doses of life's relentless challenges; however, a calm mind and inner peace will guide us through these rough patches and bring us out to the other side, where Joy awaits.

The formula for Joy, at its core, is deeply spiritual. It is remarkable how easily we can overlook it. This pathway to Joy calls for a faith-centered perspective, one that begins with a trust in God's divine master plan and the belief that His Joy is our strength (Nehemiah 8:10). Challenges are no longer seen as insurmountable obstacles but as opportunities for growth, shaping us into who God has called us to be. Setbacks become temporary detours, refining our character and deepening our dependence on Him.

Resilience is a vital component of this spiritual formula. Rooted in faith, resilience empowers us to face life's trials with purpose and determination, knowing that our Joy is not dictated by circumstances but is anchored in the unchanging nature of God's love and promises.

As you engage in this self-coaching journey, you will be called to ask yourself soul-searching questions, beginning with, "Who am I in Christ?" The answer must be truthful. Your divine identity as a beloved child of God. Authenticity is essential in this process, as it invites you to step boldly into the fullness of who God created you to be. Living in Joy means embracing your God-given uniqueness and aligning your thoughts, actions, and passions with His purpose for your life.

Ultimately, this formula for Joy is about surrender, letting go of what the world says about you, and standing firmly in the truth of who God says you are. When authenticity and faith intersect, the result is a life overflowing with the unshakable, enduring Joy that only God can provide.

The formula for Joy is simple, yet it is amazing how we can get tripped up and miss it. *Coaching Yourself on Joy* demands that you have a positive outlook on life. Challenges are viewed as opportunities for growth, and setbacks are temporary roadblocks on your journey to greater Joy. Resilience is included in the formula as well. You tackle challenges with purpose and determination instead of being overwhelmed by challenges, knowing that difficulties do not diminish Joy.

The self-coach will ask you many important questions, leading with, "Who are you?" This is wonderful because only the truth about who you are would work. The authenticity of you will step forward without any prompting when you arrive at this point in your search for Joy. You will be required to embrace your true self unapologetically. Living in your Joy means being authentic and aligning your actions with your values and passions.

There is more to consider as you seek to own your Joy. What do you believe and trust the most as a guiding force in your life? What, in other words, is your spiritual connection?

Spiritual Connection: If you have a spiritual or religious belief system, you feel a deep connection with your higher power. Your faith is a source of comfort and Joy.

Passion-Driven: You pursue your passions and engage in activities that ignite your soul. Whether it is a creative hobby, a career that aligns with your interests, or a cause you are passionate about, you find Joy in what you do.

Acts of Kindness: You engage in acts of kindness towards others and yourself. Small acts of generosity and self-compassion become daily rituals that bring you immense Joy.

Gratitude: You regularly express gratitude for the simple things in life. Whether it is a warm cup of tea, a sunrise, or a kind word from a friend, you find Joy in acknowledging life's blessings.

Mindfulness: You practice mindfulness, savoring the present moment. Whether sipping a cup of coffee, taking a leisurely walk, or simply breathing deeply, you are fully present and find Joy in the now.

Healthy Relationships: Your relationships are nourishing and filled with love and laughter. You surround yourself with people who uplift your spirit and share in your Joy.

Radiating Joy: Your Joy is contagious. Others are drawn to your positive energy, and you can uplift those around you, creating happiness.

Living in the Present: You let go of regrets about the past and anxieties about the future. You relish the present, finding Joy in each moment as it unfolds. Forgiving yourself for things and experiences that are over. This is an important must-do.

Fulfilling Purpose: You have a sense of purpose and meaning in your life. You wake up each day excited and eager to make the most of every moment.

Embracing Challenges: You view challenges as opportunities to gain experience and grow. Instead of fearing them, you approach them with curiosity and enthusiasm, trusting that you will be all right on the other side of the challenge.

When you live your Joy daily, your life becomes a tapestry of positivity, resilience, and deep satisfaction. It truly is about embracing the beauty of each moment, finding Joy in the ordinary, and cultivating a sense of fulfillment that permeates every aspect of your existence.

Living a life of Joy will elicit various responses from others, and there will be positive and negative impacts on yourself and those around you. Here are some criticisms, potential impacts, and considerations when living and owning a life of Joy:

CRITICISMS TO EXPECT:

Perceived Ignorance: Some people may perceive your Joy as ignorance or naivety, particularly if they believe you are not fully acknowledging the challenges and hardships in life.

Jealousy or Resentment: Your constant happiness may trigger jealousy or resentment in those struggling to find Joy themselves. They might wonder why you have it so easily. My response is to remind myself that most of these people do not know my story.

Dismissal of Problems: There might be a misconception that your Joyful attitude means you dismiss or trivialize serious issues, when the truth is, you are adept at facing them with resilience. People outside of your very close circle do not know the struggles you might have had to get to the mindset you are currently in.

Expectations: People might expect you to be perpetually happy and may not understand when you have moments of sadness or difficulty. The mistake that others might make is that any glimpse of sadness they see in you provides an opening for them to critique your advocacy for Joy.

POSITIVE IMPACT OF BEING JOY-FILLED:

Inspiration: Joy can inspire others, motivating them to seek Joy in their lives and adopt a more positive outlook. This is an intention that I have set for myself as a coach.

Positive Relationships: Your Joyful attitude can attract positive and like-minded individuals, fostering strong, uplifting relationships.

Emotional Contagion: Your happiness can spread to others through emotions, creating a positive atmosphere in your surroundings.

Resilience: Your ability to maintain Joy in the face of challenges can exemplify resilience and problem-solving.

JOY IN ADVERSITY

Certainly, it is crucial to acknowledge the stark contrast between the challenges that individuals in peaceful, stable environments face and those who endure the harshest conditions, marked by war, conflict, and oppressive regimes. Maintaining Joy may seem insurmountable for those living in such dire circumstances. However, the desire for Joy and the human spirit's resilience persist even in the most adverse conditions.

People living in war-torn regions or under oppressive regimes are not bereaved of the desire for Joy, peace, and fulfillment. Their longing for these positive emotions may be even more pronounced as they seek solace amidst turmoil. Pursuing Joy in such circumstances, it is a testament to the universal desire for happiness, even in the darkest times.

In the face of immense adversity, people often find Joy in:

Acts of Resilience: Resilience in the face of adversity can bring a sense of accomplishment and even Joy. The ability to withstand harsh conditions and meet each day with hope and gratitude.

Solidarity: Offering messages of solidarity and hope through letters, videos, and public poster boards can provide emotional support and a sense of connection for those who feel isolated.

Creating Safe Spaces: Establishing safe spaces for individuals to share their stories, experiences, and emotions can be crucial in healing and fostering Joy.

It is important to recognize that Joy in such circumstances may be fleeting, and the primary goal most often is survival. Yet, we can contribute to their resilience and hope by supporting these communities with resources, advocacy, and care. While it may be challenging to fathom how Joy can exist in such dire circumstances, it is a testament to the enduring human spirit and the universal desire for happiness, even in the darkest times.

Overcoming Obstacles: For those dealing with challenges like mental health issues, it may be more difficult to experience Joy. In such cases, seeking support, whether through therapy, medication, or other means, can be essential in helping individuals regain their capacity for Joy.

Variability of Joy: It is important to understand that, like all emotions, it is not a constant state. People experience a range of emotions, and Joy may come and go. It is normal to have moments or seasons of Joy along with moments or seasons of sadness, anger, or other emotions.

Individual Differences: People have various sources of Joy and different ways of experiencing it. What brings Joy to one person may not necessarily bring Joy to another.

IMPORTANT CONSIDERATIONS:

Being authentic is so important in this search for Joy. Pretending to be happy when you are not can have negative consequences on your mental health and relationships. Expressing and acknowledging moments of feeling down allows for the work necessary to maintain Joy.

It is important, however, to set boundaries that allow your vulnerability to be expressed or communicated with those close to you and willing to support you in ways that uplift and point you to the Joy you have worked hard to have.

Likewise, having and showing compassion for others going through tough times is to be mindful. Your expression of empathy and compassion for others is essential. Be aware of the assured criticisms and prepare yourself to manage them with grace and forgiveness. In my experience, these criticisms have hurt at times. However, they have not been enough to keep me from my rooted intention to be in

Joy and choose a life defined by Joy moments without denying the existence of life's challenges.

The price you pay to be a Joy-filled person is the effort and intentionality it takes to maintain your positive outlook and emotional well-being. It involves practicing self-care, embracing challenges with resilience, and nurturing meaningful relationships. While there may be criticisms and challenges along the way, the rewards of living a Joy-filled life often outweigh the costs, as it can lead to greater overall happiness, improved health, and more fulfilling relationships.

Acts of Solidarity: Coming together as a community to support one another and share resources can create moments of Joy. The bonds formed through shared struggle can be a source of comfort.

Small Moments of Relief: In difficult situations, individuals appreciate brief periods of relief, such as sharing a meal, experiencing laughter, or temporarily escaping conflict.

Cultural and Spiritual Traditions: Many individuals in challenging circumstances draw solace from their cultural and spiritual traditions. These rituals offer a sense of connection and hope.

HOW OTHERS CAN HELP

For those living in regions plagued by war, devastation, or oppressive regimes, external support can make a significant difference in their pursuit of Joy:

Humanitarian Aid: Supporting humanitarian organizations and efforts can provide essential resources, such as food, clean water, and medical care, which alleviate suffering and create opportunities for moments of Joy.

Advocacy and Awareness: Raising awareness about the challenges faced by these individuals can garner international support and put pressure on authorities to improve living conditions.

Empowerment Programs: Initiatives providing education, vocational training, and psychological support can empower individuals to regain control over their lives and find Joy through self-improvement.

In summary, Joy is a fundamental aspect of the human emotional experience. While some individuals may face obstacles in experiencing Joy, it is a state that can be cultivated, nurtured, and accessed by most people. It is a valuable and resilient emotion that can bring positivity and meaning to one's life.

AFFIRMATION ON OWNING YOUR JOY

I claim my Joy's ownership; it is my birthright
and divine inheritance.

I release all dependencies on external circumstances or others to
define my happiness.

Joy flows from within me, rooted in the unshakable foundation of my
faith, purpose, and self-love. I choose to see beauty and gratitude in
every moment, no matter how small or fleeting.

Even in the face of challenges, I am steadfast in my commitment to
nurture and protect my Joy. I honor my spirit by embracing what
uplifts me and letting go of what no longer serves me.

Joy is my power, my peace, and my strength. Today and every day, I
own my Joy unapologetically and share its light with the world.

A PRAYER FOR OWNING YOUR JOY.

Dear God,

I have asked that the words of my mouth and the meditation of my heart be acceptable in your sight. My trust in you and belief in the power of prayer cause me to pause here and offer a prayer for those who would read these words of encouragement.

You are the source from which every perfect gift flows. We come before You, as individuals and as a community, seeking to root ourselves in the deep and abiding Joy that comes from knowing You.

Teach us, Lord, to look beyond fleeting pleasures and temporary satisfactions. Help us to see that true Joy is found not in what we possess but in who You are. Open our hearts to experience the fullness of Your presence, for in Your presence is the fullness of Joy.

As individuals, guide us to reflect on Your goodness daily. Let us find Joy in the quiet moments through gratitude for the sunrise, the comfort of Your Word, and the beauty of relationships You have placed around us. May we grow in the assurance that You work all things together for good, even in seasons of challenge and loss.

As a group, unite us in a shared vision of Joy that uplifts and strengthens each community member. Let us encourage one another with words of hope, acts of kindness, and the reminder of Your steadfast love. Teach us to celebrate together, to weep together, and to serve one another with glad hearts. May our collective Joy be a testimony of Your transforming power to the world around us.

Lord, help us to center our lives on Jesus, the Joy of our salvation and the anchor of our souls. May His example inspire us to live with humility, grace, and the unshakable hope of eternity with You.

Fill us with the Joy that surpasses all understanding, a Joy that overflows and blesses others. May it shine through us as a light in the darkness, pointing others to You, the ultimate source of Joy.

In Jesus' precious name, we pray. Amen.

Write ways you will own your own Joy

_____

_____

_____

_____

_____

_____

_____

_____

_____

_____

_____

_____

_____

_____

_____

_____

_____

COACHING YOURSELF ON JOY

5

CHAPTER

An Essay on
Sharing Your Joy

5

SHARING YOUR JOY

"You make known to me the path of life; you will fill me with Joy in your presence, with eternal pleasures at your right hand."

Psalm 16:11

"What counts in life is not the mere fact that we have lived. It is what difference we have made to the lives of others that will determine the significance of the life we lead."

—Nelson Mandela

PURPOSE AND LEGACY

One day, I was having a special conversation with my six-year-old grandson, Emir. We talked about all sorts of things, following his curious little mind wherever it led. But my main goal was to help him get ready for a big change; moving out of our home, where he had lived with us and his mom, Kelsey, during the COVID-19 shutdown.

For almost a year, Emir had been sleeping in our bed because he was afraid to sleep alone in his own room. Now, he and his mom were moving into their own apartment, and I wanted to help him see this transition as something exciting rather than scary.

I gently asked, "Are you excited about having your own room in your new home with Mommy?"

His face lit up. At just six years old, he was already imagining the Joy of being with his mommy, just the two of them. To him, this move meant having a special space that belonged only to them, a place where their love and connection would only grow and the fun of it all was something special to look forward to.

As he shared his excitement, I knew that my message and intent for this conversation were being met. I wanted to help him embrace this new chapter with Joy-filled dreams, seeing his new home as a wonderful adventure rather than something to fear.

Sharing my stories, each one landing on a message of victory, is a legacy I deeply cherish. At sixty-seven, I have the great fortune and blessing of being in a reflective season of life, where I can fully embrace the present while drawing wisdom from the past. With every story I tell, I see the triumph in each challenge and the richness of a life deeply engaged in purpose.

My journey has never followed a conventional path. From an early age, I made bold choices, often stepping beyond what was expected of me. I moved through life guided by faith, courage, and a willingness to embrace the unknown. These decisions shaped a life filled with surprises, unconventional experiences, and the kind of wisdom that can only be gained by walking a road less traveled.

Now, as I share my stories, I do so with Joy knowing that each one holds the power to inspire, uplift, and remind others that victory is always within reach.

A JOURNEY TO LOVE AND PARTNERSHIP

At just twenty-one, I entered a loving marriage with an incredible human being that, while lasting only seven years, led me to the greatest blessing of my life, Stanley Perkins, my soulmate and life partner. With Stanley, I experienced the true Joys of partnership. Together, we learned how to be a couple, became best friends, and grew into loving parents, business partners, and unwavering supporters of each other.

Marriage became the foundation of our journey, but we made a conscious decision to infuse it with Joy. We did not have many examples of Joyful marriages growing up, but we believed we could create a new model, one that would inspire our children and grandchildren. For forty years, we have been sharing the Joys of love, commitment, and family. This was our greatest gift given and received.

Telling this story brings me Joy because it is a testament to what's possible when two people choose love, friendship, and a shared vision for a life filled with happiness.

CREATING A LEGACY OF SUCCESS

Some believe Stanley and I redefined our family dynamics. Both our mothers were hard-working, no-nonsense mothers who, for different reasons, had to raise their children as single mothers. Stanley's mom had three boys and four girls, and my mother had four girls and six boys. Life was a struggle, particularly financially. However, we both share canvases of Joy when painting a verbal picture of the stories of our lives growing up, because we tell our stories from the perspective of victory. We both were overcomers who came from families where our mothers demonstrated that type of victory.

Through hard work and determination, we transformed our lives from "barely making it" to an upper-middle-class family. We did not stop with just us; we shared our achievements with extended family, inspiring them to reach out and dream new and bigger dreams.

LIFE OF IMPACT

Looking back on my journey, I see the profound impact that mentorship has had, not just on me, but on the lives I have touched as a life coach and mentor for over twenty-five years. Mentoring is one of the most powerful ways to shape the next generation, both within families and in the broader community. It is my way of giving back, honoring those who invested their time and wisdom in me.

My life has been shaped by remarkable women, starting with my mother, whose sacrifices I did not fully understand as a child. She gave me all that she had and then made the difficult decision to send me to live with my great-grand aunt, Kathleen Marshall, so I could receive even more. At the time, I felt hurt by this decision and could not appreciate it, but as I grew older, I realized what a tremendous gift it was, an act of love that set me on a path of growth and purpose.

In adulthood, I was blessed with another transformative mentor: Dr. Dorothy Irene Height. Meeting her in 1991, at the age of 31, marked the beginning of a life-changing relationship. She was the first mentor I had outside of my family, and she modeled leadership, service, and the power of lifting others as you climb.

Another defining influence in my journey was Iyanla Vanzant. Through her coaching, I saw the power of transformation firsthand, not just in theory, but in practice. She modeled what it meant to guide others with wisdom, compassion, and unwavering belief in their potential. Iyanla's example inspired me to become a life coach, dedicating my life to helping others step into their greatness.

Now, as I reflect, I see my legacy not just in my own accomplishments, but in the people I have mentored, the lives I have touched, and the ripple effect of empowerment that continues to spread. Mentorship has been the thread weaving together generations of wisdom, love, and purpose, and I am honored to be both a recipient and a giver of that sacred gift.

OVERCOMING CHALLENGES

My life has been defined by perseverance, overcoming significant challenges at every stage. For nearly seven decades, each era of my life has presented a major hurdle, yet I have faced them all with faith and determination.

At just five years old, I found myself stuck on a window ledge in Overtown, Miami, a terrifying moment that left an early imprint of fear and survival. A year later, I experienced the first death and deep loss of my grandfather, my first teacher and protector, leaving me confused and unsure of the world. Soon after, I was sent to live with his aunt, Kathleen, in another country, separated from the family and familiar surroundings that had been my foundation. Navigating that sudden displacement was one of my earliest and most profound challenges. It was almost too much to ask of a child.

Adulthood brought its own battles. The fight to save both my babies and me during childbirth left permanent physical and emotional scars, reshaping my understanding of strength and sacrifice. Then came a devastating diagnosis, stage three breast cancer, a battle I fought and won, emerging with a deeper appreciation for life and purpose. Years later, I faced yet another life-threatening trial, a severe case of COVID-19 in the early days of the pandemic, a time when so many did not survive. I beat those odds, restoration defining my life.

Perhaps one of the longest-running challenges I carried was the pursuit of my doctorate. After twenty-five years of starting and stopping, wrestling with obstacles that delayed my progress, I finally completed the journey. It was not just an academic achievement; it is proof of my unwavering commitment to finishing whatever I had begun.

Through it all, my faith and resilience have been my guiding forces. No matter how difficult the road is, I have always chosen to rise, to heal, and to move forward in Joy. These challenges have not defined me; rather, they have refined me, shaping the woman I am today.

THE QUEST FOR JOY

I cannot pinpoint exactly when my quest for Joy began, but I know that life's extreme highs and lows have always presented me with a choice. Through every challenge and triumph, I have chosen Joy not just for myself, but also as a gift to others and as a lasting part of my legacy.

Pursuing Joy and helping others do the same is my life's commitment. I see it as my sacred assignment to embrace as much Joy as my heart can hold and to share that Joy so that it continues to ripple long after I am gone. My story is one of transformation, resilience, and an unyielding faith in the power of Joy to heal, uplift, and inspire.

Coaching Yourself on Joy is more than a book; it is an offering of wisdom and experience, a guide to help you, the reader, discover ways to invite more Joy into your life. My deepest hope is that it inspires you to follow your heart, rise above adversity, and cherish the Joy that life has to offer.

Joy is my choice, my purpose, and my legacy.

A LIFE GUIDED BY FAITH AND INTENTION

"For I know the plans I have for you," declares the Lord, "plans to prosper you and not to harm you, plans to give you hope and a future."

Jeremiah 29:11 (NIV)

Laurie Lee Gipson (mum) stood up with me in Faith Temple Church of God to become my Godmother when I was ten. She believed in the invisible, at least to the naked eye, power of prayer and faith for the fifty-seven years we have been together. Today, at eighty-three years old, she continues inserting faith in every conversation we have.

A central theme for my life has been,

"I can do all things through Christ who strengthens me."

I trust that in this guide, the importance of faith, intention, and personal empowerment will resonate with you, dear reader.

Allow my story to be a testament to the limitless potential within everyone and how, with faith and intentionality, anyone can shape their destiny and discover the true Joy life has to offer.

I want my legacy to be a beacon of inspiration for all who come across these words. Take what resonates with you, and feel free to share these messages with others. They deserve Joy, too!

AFFIRMATION ON SHARING JOY

I am a vessel of Joy and delight in sharing it freely with the world.

The Joy within me grows stronger and brighter as
I extend it to others.

I uplift and inspire those around me through my words,
actions, and presence.

I share my Joy with an open heart, knowing it can heal,
connect, and transform.

In giving Joy, I create a ripple effect of love, kindness, and positivity.

I trust that the Joy I share will multiply and return to me in beautiful
and unexpected ways.

My Joy is abundant, unselfish, and infinite, a gift meant to be shared
with grace and intention. Together, we create a world filled with
light, hope, and boundless Joy.

A PRAYER FOR SHARING JOY

Dear Heavenly Father,

Thank You for the abundant Joy You have poured into my life, a Joy that flows from Your love and faithfulness. Today, I come to You with a heart filled with gratitude and a desire to share this gift with others.

Lord, help me to be a vessel of Joy, radiating Your light and love wherever I go. Let my words bring encouragement, my actions offer kindness, and my presence inspire hope. May the Joy You have placed within me bless those around me, lifting spirits and brightening lives.

Teach me to recognize the opportunities to share Joy, even in the smallest ways: a kind word, a thoughtful gesture, or a listening ear. Help me see beyond my own needs and reach out with compassion to those who may be struggling or need a reminder of Your goodness.

Father, remind me that sharing Joy is an act of worship, a way to reflect Your grace and glory to the world. Let my happiness be contagious, sparking hope in hearts that feel heavy and illuminating paths that feel dark.

Thank You for equipping me with the ability to spread Joy and trusting me to reflect Your love. May I always seek to uplift others and remind them of the pleasure of knowing You.

Amen.

Write how you are sharing your Joy.

_____

_____

_____

_____

_____

_____

_____

_____

_____

_____

_____

_____

_____

_____

_____

_____

_____

6

CHAPTER

*An Essay on
Fixating on Joy*

6

FIXATING ON JOY

"Faith, who for the Joy set before Him endured the cross."

Hebrews 12:2

"My Joy is not for others to validate; it is my testament to the God I believe and serve. My Joy is my story, my testimony, my evidence of his goodness in my life."

—Coach Barbara A. Perkins

FIXATE ON JOY: A CALLING, NOT JUST A FEELING

To fixate on Joy means to make it the center of your life, your thoughts, actions, and faith. It is a conscious decision to focus on the goodness of God, no matter the circumstances, and to let Joy guide your journey. This is not a passive feeling that comes and goes; it is an intentional way of living, rooted in faith and strengthened by trust in God's plan.

But why fixate on Joy? Because the Bible makes it clear that Joy is essential to our spiritual lives. It is mentioned over three hundred times in scripture,while *happiness* appears only about thirty times. This distinction is powerful. Joy is not something fleeting or dependent on external conditions. It is a divine gift, a source of strength, and a testimony of our relationship with God.

Yet, one of the greatest obstacles to Joy is fear. The Bible's most repeated command is *"Fear not."* Fear has the power to cloud our faith, distract us from our purpose, and steal the Joy that God intends for us. When we choose to fixate on Joy, we reject fear's influence and stand firm in the assurance that we are never alone.

Living a life fixated on Joy also means being a light for others. In a world that often glorifies stress, struggle, and cynicism, choosing Joy is a radical act. Society encourages passion for sports, entertainment, and activism, but unwavering Joy is often misunderstood. Some may see it as unrealistic or even naïve. But as believers, we know that Joy is not just an emotion—it is a fruit of the Spirit, a reflection of faith, and a powerful witness to God's presence in our lives.

Fixating on Joy is more than a personal pursuit; it is a calling. It is a choice to live in alignment with God's promises, to embrace Joy as a foundation rather than a fleeting feeling, and to leave a legacy of faith, light, and unwavering trust in His goodness.

THE BIBLICAL CALL TO JOY

The Bible's emphasis on Joy is no accident. Joy is a marker of God's Presence, a signal of His work in our lives. Psalm 16:11 declares,

"You make known to me the path of life; you will fill me with Joy in your presence."

This verse reminds us that Joy is not found in external circumstances but God's Presence. To be fixated on Joy is to fix our gaze on God.

The juxtaposition between Joy and fear is also no coincidence. Fear is the great interrupter of Joy. When fear dominates our thoughts, it crowds out the peace and assurance that Joy brings. This is why Scripture repeatedly tells us to "fear not." Fear is a natural emotion, but unchecked, it becomes a barrier between us and the fullness of Joy God intends for us to experience.

THE COURAGE TO BE JOYFUL

Being fixated on Joy takes courage. It means resisting the pressure to downplay your Joy to make others comfortable. It means choosing Joy even when circumstances suggest otherwise. It means letting your Joy shine as a reflection of God's glory, knowing that it is not dependent on the approval or understanding of others.

Joy is contagious. When you allow your Joy to radiate freely, it inspires others to seek Joy in their lives. Think about the people in your life who exude Joy, their presence is uplifting, their energy magnetic. This is not because they have perfect lives but because they have chosen to let Joy be their testimony.

JOY AS YOUR BRAND AND CALLING CARD

Imagine if Joy were your brand, something you are known for, a consistent theme in how you live, work, and interact with others. How would your life change? How would your relationships deepen? How would your faith grow?

When you are fixated on Joy, it shows in everything you do. Your words carry encouragement. Your actions reflect kindness. Your attitude inspires hope. People are drawn to you, not because you have all the answers, but because your Joy reminds them of God's goodness.

In Philippians 4:4, Paul writes,

"Rejoice in the Lord always. I will say it again: Rejoice!"

This command is not a suggestion or occasional practice but a lifestyle. To rejoice is to choose Joy, fixate on it, and let it permeate every aspect of your being.

PRACTICAL WAYS TO FIXATE ON JOY

1. **Begin Your Day with Gratitude**
   Start each day by listing three things for which you are grateful. Gratitude is a gateway to Joy. It shifts your focus from what you lack to what you have, opening your heart to God's blessings.

2. **Surround Yourself with Joyful People**
   Joy is contagious. Spend time with people who uplift and inspire you, encourage your faith, and remind you of God's goodness.

3. **Celebrate the Small Things**
   Joy is not reserved for major milestones. Find Joy in everyday moments, a kind word, a beautiful sunset, a laugh with a friend.

4. **Guard Your Heart Against Fear**
   Fear disrupts Joy. When fear arises, confront it with faith. Speak scripture over your life and remind yourself of God's promises.

5. **Share Your Joy**
   Joy multiplies when shared. Be intentional about spreading Joy to others through a smile, a kind gesture, or words of encouragement. Let your Joy reflect God's love.

OVERCOMING THE FEAR OF JUDGMENT

If you have ever hesitated to express your Joy for fear of being judged or misunderstood, remember this: Your Joy is not for others to validate; it is a testament to the God you serve. Your Joy is your story, testimony, and evidence of His goodness.

Yes, some may call you overzealous. But isn't God worth our zeal? If we can be passionate about things in this world, how much more passionate should we be about the Joy of knowing Him?

CONCLUSION: BE UNAPOLOGETICALLY JOYFUL

To fixate on Joy is to live unapologetically in the fullness of God's promises. It is to let your life reflect its goodness, even in difficult times. Joy is not just a gift to be received; it is a calling to be lived out.

So, rejoice boldly. Live passionately. Let your Joy shine as a beacon of hope and faith. Be fixated on Joy; let it be your testimony to the world.

Joy is your birthright. Claim it. Live it. Share it.

AFFIRMATION OF BEING FIXATED ON JOY

I fix my heart and mind on Joy, making it the center of my existence.

Joy is my focus, anchor, and guide, no matter what
unfolds around me.

I am fixed in my commitment to seek Joy in every
experience, big or small.

Challenges may come, but my fixation on Joy empowers me to rise
above them with grace.

My thoughts are filled with positivity, my actions are aligned with
love, and my spirit is devoted to peace.

I am resolute in choosing Joy, which fuels my soul and
brightens my path.

Being fixated on Joy allows me to create a life of abundance,
fulfillment, and harmony.

I hold onto Joy tightly, knowing it is my divine compass to a life of
purpose and happiness.

A PRAYER ABOUT BEING FIXATED ON JOY

Dear Heavenly Father,

Thank You for being the source of my Joy, the foundation of my peace, and the anchor of my hope. Today, I come to You with a heart yearning to stay fixated on the Joy You have placed within me.

Lord, help me to keep my eyes focused on You and the blessings that flow from Your love. When the storms of life threaten to distract or discourage me, remind me that Your Joy is unshakable and ever-present. Strengthen me to rise above negativity, fear, and doubt and to cling to the peace that surpasses all understanding.

Teach me to recognize beauty in every moment, to savor the gifts You place before me, and to remain steadfast in gratitude. Let my Joy not waver with circumstances but be rooted in the eternal truth of Your presence.

Guide my thoughts, Father, so they align with Your will and bring light and positivity into my life. May my heart be so fixated on the Joy that it overflows into every interaction, uplifting others and glorifying You.

Help me let go of anything that will rob me of my Joy. Replace my worries with trust, my doubts with faith, and my sorrows with the assurance that You are always with me.

Thank You, Lord, for being my source of Joy, comfort, and guidance. I trust you to keep my heart steadfast, my spirit lifted, and my focus fixed on the Joy that comes from living in Your love.

In Jesus' name, I pray. Amen.

Write how will you fixate on JOY

7

CHAPTER

*An Essay on the
Levitating in Joy*

7

LEVITATING IN JOY

"But they that wait upon the Lord shall renew their strength; they shall mount up with wings as eagles; they shall run, and not be weary; and they shall walk, and not faint."

Isaiah 40:31

"Once I realized the pain and grief from losing my precious son, my only child was not going to kill me, I found my Joy again . . . "

LaTosha Brown

It is with intention that I have repeated this phrase throughout these essays, "Joy is a gift from God." It was intended for us to read it repeatedly. The gift of Joy, a divine state that transcends circumstances and remains anchored in God's promises, is available to us even though life is filled with situations, challenges, and people who can attempt to steal this Joy from us.

Disappointments, hardships, losses, and even everyday routine frustrations have a way of interrupting our Joy and our peace. To truly experience Joy as a way of being, we must learn to rise above these Joy busters. We must learn to *levitate in Joy*, to lift ourselves, through faith, above the weight of negativity and discouragement.

THE CALL TO RISE ABOVE

The Bible often speaks of overcoming life's challenges and finding strength in God. Isaiah 40:31 reminds us, *"But they that wait upon the Lord shall renew their strength; they shall mount up with wings as eagles; they shall run, and not be weary; and they shall walk, and not faint."* This verse illustrates that our strength, our ability to rise, comes not from our power but from trusting and waiting on the Lord.

To levitate in Joy is to ascend spiritually and emotionally above the trials of life, keeping our focus on God's goodness and unwavering promises. It does not mean ignoring challenges or pretending they do not exist. Rather, it means refusing to allow them to keep us in despair and hopelessness.

THE NATURE OF JOY-BUSTERS

Joy-busters come in many forms: fear, doubt, comparison, envy, grief, and even the opinions of others. They seek to weigh us down, to distract us from God's presence, and to disrupt our peace.

In John 10:10, Jesus said,

"The thief comes only to steal and kill and destroy; I have come that they may have life and have it to the full."

This thief can represent anything that disrupts the abundant life Jesus promises, including our Joy. To levitate in Joy, we must identify these thieves and refuse to let them take hold. In identifying the Joy thieves, we must first look in the not-so-obvious spaces, such as our minds and hearts. What false narratives are we holding onto? What have we made up in our minds? What non-serving evidence are we maintaining, saving to prove the erroneous beliefs about ourselves? Start within as a first step to finding the Joy-busters and stealers of our hopes and dreams.

JOY AND MENTAL WELLNESS

Learning to levitate in Joy has profound implications for mental health. Depression, anxiety, and other emotional ills often thrive in environments of despair, fear, and unresolved stress. By intentionally focusing on God's Joy, we create a spiritual and emotional shield that helps us combat these negative forces.

Proverbs 17:22 says,

"A cheerful heart is good medicine, but a crushed spirit dries up the bones."

This verse reminds us of the healing power of Joy, not just spiritually, physically, and emotionally. When we elevate our minds and hearts above the challenges of life, we create space for God's peace to guard us against anxiety (Philippians 4:6-7) and depression.

BIBLICAL PRINCIPLES FOR LEVITATING IN JOY

1. **Keep Your Focus on God**

    Hebrews 12:2 encourages us to focus on Jesus, *"the author and finisher of our faith."* We are lifted above the world's noise when we focus on Him. Much like Peter walking on water (Matthew 14:28-31), we rise if our gaze remains on Jesus. When we shift our focus to the rough waves, our problems begin to sink.

2. **Cast Your Burdens on the Lord**

    Psalm 55:22 tells us to *"Cast your burden on the Lord, and He will sustain you."* We must let go of what weighs us down to levitate in Joy. This is not avoidance but a spiritual act of surrender. Trusting God with our burdens allows us to rise above them.

3. **Choose Praise Over Complaints**

    Praise has a lifting power. When Paul and Silas were imprisoned, they sang hymns to God (Acts 16:25-26). Their Joy-filled praise shook the prison's foundations, leading to their freedom. Praise transforms our perspective and elevates our spirits, helping us to rise above even the most confining and difficult situations.

4.   **Guard Your Heart and Mind**
Proverbs 4:23 says,

"Above all else, guard your heart, for everything you do flows from it."

To levitate in Joy, we must protect our inner peace. This means being mindful of what we consume, the people we surround ourselves with, and the thoughts we entertain. Philippians 4:8 reminds us to think about whatever is true, noble, right, pure, lovely, and admirable.

5.   **Rely on the Holy Spirit**
The Holy Spirit is our helper and guide, equipping us to rise above earthly struggles. Galatians 5:22-23 lists Joy as a fruit of the Spirit. When we walk in the Spirit, we are empowered to live in Joy, no matter what comes our way.

PRACTICAL STEPS TO LEVITATING IN JOY

1.   **Anchor Yourself in Scripture**
Memorize and meditate on verses that affirm God's promises of Joy. Let His Word be the foundation that lifts you above life's challenges.

2.   **Practice Gratitude Daily**
Gratitude is a powerful antidote to negativity. By focusing on what you have rather than your lack, you elevate your spirit and align your heart with God's blessings.

COACHING YOURSELF ON JOY

3. **Let Go of What You Cannot Control.**
    Release the need to control every situation or outcome. Trust that God is in control and works for your good (Romans 8:28).

4. **Stay in Worship and Prayer**
    Worship lifts your heart and mind into God's Presence. In prayer, you exchange your burdens for His peace, helping you to rise above difficulties.

5. **Surround Yourself with Uplifting Community**
    Joy is contagious. Surround yourself with people who uplift, encourage, and inspire you. Their Joy will help you rise when you feel weighed down.

6. **Get Creative and Child-Like**
    Remembering when you were a child full of innocence and Joy, re-imagine those times and incorporate them into your life. I am not suggesting becoming childish, but to be okay with child-like Joy.

A BIBLICAL EXAMPLE: NEHEMIAH AND THE JOY OF THE LORD

In Nehemiah 8:10, the prophet declared,

"The Joy of the Lord is your strength."

This declaration came during a time of rebuilding and renewal for the Israelites. Despite their challenges, Nehemiah reminded them to find their strength in the Joy of the Lord.

Their Joy was not based on their circumstances but on their relationship with God. Similarly, when we place our faith in God, we can experience Joy that sustains us and allows us to rise above anything that seeks to pull us down.

ASCEND TO JOY

To levitate in Joy is understanding that God's Joy is always available to you. It is to choose Joy daily, to protect it fiercely, and to allow it to lift you above life's trials. Learning to levitate in Joy shields you from the heavy burdens of anxiety, depression, and other emotional struggles. It aligns your heart with God's peace, which surpasses all understanding (Philippians 4:7).

As you face life's challenges, hold on to the truth that Joy is your strength. Like an eagle soaring above the storm, you can rise above anything that seeks to steal your Joy. Trust in God, cast your cares on Him, and allow His Spirit to lift you to new heights.

> *"You will keep in perfect peace those whose minds are steadfast, because they trust in You."*
>
> Isaiah 26:3

Joy is your inheritance. Levitate above the trials and let the Joy of the Lord be your strength and your song.

AFFIRMATION ON LEVITATING TO REMAIN IN JOY

I rise above all that seeks to pull me away from my Joy.
I am weightless and free, unburdened by negativity, doubt, or fear.

Like a gentle breeze lifting me higher, I levitate above challenges,
choosing Joy as my sanctuary.

No matter the circumstances, I ascend to a place of
peace, grace, and light.

I release the heaviness of worry and allow my spirit to soar, anchored
in the power of Joy.

The higher I rise, the clearer my perspective becomes, and I see only
the beauty and blessings of life.

I am untouchable in my Joy, elevated by faith, gratitude, and love.

With every breath, I ascend, effortlessly maintaining the Joy, which
is my divine birthright.

A PRAYER ON LEVITATING TO REMAIN IN JOY

Dear Heavenly Father,

Thank You for the gift of Joy, a sacred and divine blessing that uplifts my spirit and strengthens my heart. Today, I ask for Your guidance to rise above anything that seeks to steal my Joy or weigh me down.

Lord, help me levitate spiritually above negativity, fear, and spiritual doubt. Lift me to a higher place where peace, gratitude, and faith sustain me. May I rise above the world's noise and remain in the light of Your presence, where Joy is abundant and unshakable.

Teach me to recognize the power You have given me to choose Joy, no matter my challenges. Remind me, Lord, that I have the strength to transcend obstacles, setbacks, and worries with You. Please fill me with a divine perspective that allows me to see every situation through the lens of hope and possibility.

As I ascend into Joy, may my heart remain light, my mind clear, and my soul anchored in Your love. Please help me to stay focused on what truly matters, releasing all burdens and distractions that do not serve my higher purpose.

Father, I trust in Your power to keep me elevated, surrounded by Your peace, and filled with the Joy only You can provide. Let my happiness inspire others, serving as a testimony of Your grace and goodness.

Thank You for lifting me higher and teaching me to remain in a place of unwavering Joy. I rest in Your promise to sustain me, now and always.

This is my prayer, Amen.

Levitating on JOY

_____

_____

_____

_____

_____

_____

_____

_____

_____

_____

_____

_____

_____

_____

_____

_____

_____

JOY:
A DIVINE MELODY

Anonymous Author

In the Spirit's fruit, it finds its place,
A gift of God, a touch of grace.
Through trials deep, it brightly glows,
A holy flame that ever grows.
From salvation's well, it springs anew,
A river flowing, pure and true.
The burdened soul, now reconciled,
Leaps with Joy, like a freed child.
In God's presence, fullness abides,
A Joy eternal that never hides.
Through worship sweet and fellowship dear,
Its melody rings for all to hear.
Not bound by earth, nor fleeting bliss,
But anchored in promises never amiss.
For heaven's glory and Christ's embrace,
Bring Joy unending, full of grace.
A radiant hope, through life and strife,
Joy stands as the anthem of eternal life
.From doctrine deep, this truth takes flight,
Joy is the believer's everlasting light.

COACHING
YOURSELF
ON
JOY

TEN POINT JOY CHECK LIST

Coach Barbara's 10-point faith-based checklist for finding, living, sharing, and maintaining Joy. This checklist is to help you navigate the daily challenges regardless of the disparities present. Incorporate these ideas that will help you rise above external hardships.

1. **Faith-Centered Foundation:** Build your Joy on a solid foundation of faith and spirituality, drawing strength from your beliefs and trust in a higher power.

2. **Self-Compassion:** Practice self-compassion and self-love, recognizing that you are worthy of Joy and happiness, regardless of external challenges.

3. **Cultivate Resilience:** Embrace resilience in the face of adversity, acknowledging that your ability to bounce back from challenges is a source of inner strength that will lead to Joy.

4. **Seek Community and Support:** Surround yourself with a supportive community that understands your

experiences and shares your journey, fostering a sense of belonging.

5. **Kindness and Empathy:** Extend kindness and empathy to others, as acts of generosity and compassion can bring you Joy and strengthen connections with others.

6. **Purpose and Service:** Find purpose in serving others and contributing to your community. Making a positive impact on others can be a source of immense Joy.

7. **Mindfulness and Gratitude:** Practice mindfulness and cultivate gratitude, cherishing the small, everyday moments that bring you Joy and focusing on the positive aspects of your life.

8. **Celebrate Achievements:** Acknowledge and celebrate your achievements, no matter how small. These moments of success can fuel your Joy and motivation.

9. **Advocate for Change:** Channel your courage to advocate for change and equity, taking action to address disparities and discrimination, which can lead to a sense of empowerment and Joy.

10. **Chart Your Path:** Recognize that your path to Joy may differ. Do not compare yourself to external standards. Your journey is uniquely yours.

"Give thanks in all circumstances; for this is God's will for you in Christ Jesus."

1 Thessalonians 5:18 (NIV)

One of my favorite songs about Joy is *What a Wonderful World*, written by George David Weiss and Bob Thiele and recorded by Louis Armstrong in 1967. The lyrics remind us to appreciate the beauty around us: "I see trees of green, red roses too / I see them bloom for me and you." These words encourage me to find Joy in everyday moments.

PERSONAL JOY STATEMENT (WRITE YOURS)

"To bestow on them a crown of beauty instead of ashes, the oil of Joy instead of mourning, and a garment of praise instead of a spirit of despair."

Isaiah 61:3

I have learned that simplicity is not always easy in my life journey. The fight for Joy is worth waging, and I proudly embrace this responsibility as my own. I understand that Joy is not a task to delegate to someone else but a flame that I must ignite and protect. I have realized that there is an invisible conspiracy, an unseen force that seeks to steal away our Joy. Therefore, I choose to stand strong, fight, and hold onto my Joy, a precious gift I am determined to cherish.

I remember being a happy, carefree five-year-old girl who loved playing outdoors with my two brothers and boy cousin. Everything felt right about the fun we had, playing with marbles in the dirt, knocking fruit from the trees in and around our yard, staying outside until the streetlights came on, and without being able to tell time, we knew the time to return home. There is no question in my mind that those times were Joy-filled, and we embodied Joy. We were the Joy carriers. Then it seemed like, in an instant, Joy went away.

I witnessed my first unexplained death at six years old, which led to my being sent away from a full house of people, both adults and children, a loud and bustlingly exciting home in the US, to a very quiet, not even a television, two-person home that I shared with my Great Grand Aunt in the Bahamas. The death of my grandfather, who was the head of the household, changed everything for me. With no real sense of time or seasons, I was suddenly in a world of silence with minimal laughter, no loud boys to play in the dirt with, and a lifestyle drastically different from the one I had.

I remember vividly meeting fear for the first time at six years old. I knew it was the first time because, at five, according to my sister Debra, I had no fear climbing onto the ledge of our window multiple stories up in our Florida apartment to retrieve a penny I had dropped from the window. The memorable evening that fear grabbed hold of me and would not let me go for years was my first night in the Bahamas when my dear, sweet Aunt Kathleen took me by the hand and led me through the dark in the back of the house to go to the outside toilet.

The old wooden building with a single latch itself was scary, but the walk to the building was worse than that. This evening ritual lasted until I was in my double digits. Daily fear wore over me like a blanket night after night. This was bad enough and big enough to shadow any small resemblance of Joy over, yet there were more and more and more cultural norms and changes that came with my new lifestyle. It was not long before I decided to seek out survival and protect myself as best as possible. I realized that all the things that made me smile and laugh as a five-year-old were potentially gone and replaced by new things.

Under the careful and strict supervision of Aunt Kathleen, I learned to fear most engagements with adults, and those I did not fear, I did not trust completely. The Joy became buried down inside. I had to bury it to preserve it for another time and space. I became a survivor at an early age, learning how to have transactional moments of happiness that were most often tied to a consequence or something I had to give.

Getting back to the authenticity of Joy took years!

It took work from the inside; it took faith and belief that a bigger plan was in place for my life. It took witnessing the Joy I saw in the lives of others that inspire me to become a Joy carrier once again. With maturity in my faith walk and belief in the Word of God, the promises He made to those who would believe in Him and follow the path He has laid out for us, I could begin to trust again. To have Joy we must have trust that it is available and available to us. What do you believe? Is Joy available to you fully and without conditions shaped by human interactions? Do you remember when and where you lost your Joy? Are you ready to have that Joy back? What is the price we pay for Joy?

"Trust in the Lord with all your heart and lean not on your own understanding."

Proverbs 3:5 (NIV)

I want to ensure that the key lessons from my story are not missed. The main messages are:

1. **The Resilience of Joy**

   Although Joy was buried deep within me, it was never extinguished. My survival instincts helped me adapt to my circumstances, but faith and the belief in a greater purpose for my life eventually unearthed my Joy. This taught me that Joy is resilient. It may lie dormant, but it is never fully lost.

2. **The Power of Witnessing Joy in Others**

   Seeing Joy in the lives of others became a beacon of hope for me. It inspired me to seek Joy again and reminded me that reclaiming what I thought had been taken from me was possible.

3. **Faith as the Foundation for Joy**

   Through maturity in my faith walk, I discovered the promises of God as a source of trust and Joy. Joy became accessible not through fleeting, conditional moments but through the unwavering assurance of God's presence and His plan for my life.

4. **The Cost of Transactional Joy**

   For years, I experienced happiness only as a transaction tied to what I could give or do. I learned that true Joy does not require payment or permission. It is a divine gift, freely available when we trust in God and embrace it as our birthright.

5. **The Journey Back to Authentic Joy**

   Reclaiming Joy required work from the inside out. It demanded faith, self-reflection, and an intentional choice to let go of fear and mistrust. It was not an instant process but a gradual journey of rediscovering my identity and divine purpose.

Write Your Joy Statement:

_____

_____

_____

_____

_____

_____

_____

_____

_____

_____

_____

_____

_____

_____

_____

_____

_____

Personal Joy Statement (Write Yours)

Personal Joy Statement (Write Yours)

_____

_____

_____

_____

_____

_____

_____

_____

_____

_____

_____

_____

_____

_____

_____

_____

_____

CONCLUSION

JOY IS WORTH THE JOURNEY

Joy is worth the journey. It is worth every step, every tear, every prayer, and every moment of self-discovery. If it takes a lifetime to experience the fullness of Joy truly, then let it be your life's work. Why not dedicate yourself to being a "work in progress" in pursuing Joy? There is no higher calling than to live in alignment with the divine gift of Joy that God has placed within each of us.

Faith and a relationship with God are the cornerstone of transforming Joy from a fleeting emotion into a sustainable way of being. Joy is not dependent on our circumstances but rooted in our Creator. When we trust in God and align our lives with His promises, Joy becomes more than a feeling; it becomes a state of being.

Through faith, we are reminded that Joy is not something we must chase endlessly; it is something we are invited to receive. Psalm 30:5 tells us that "weeping may endure for a night, but Joy comes in the morning." This is not just poetic imagery; it is a divine promise that Joy is always on the horizon when we walk with God.

A relationship with God transforms how we see the world and ourselves. It allows us to view challenges not as Joy stealers but as opportunities for growth and deeper reliance on Him. It teaches us that Joy is not the absence of pain but the presence of peace, hope, and trust in God's plan. Faith makes Joy sustainable because it anchors us to something eternal.

As you reflect on this journey, I hope this guide will be a road map, a guide to discovering, choosing, and remaining in Joy. I pray that it will challenge you to see Joy as more than an elusive dream but a destination worth striving for. The search for Joy is not easy, but it is always worth it. It is a journey of faith, letting go of fear, and embracing the truth that Joy is your birthright, your inheritance as a child of God.

So, I ask you now, why not let Joy be your life's work? Why not let Joy be your legacy for your family, community, and the world? Why not commit to being a "work in progress" in Joy? Allow God to shape and mold you into who He created you to be. Why not be someone who carries Joy not just in their heart but in their actions, words, and presence?

As you continue this path, hold fast to this truth: Joy is worth it. You are worth it. God has equipped you with everything you need to experience and sustain Joy.

May your life be a testimony to the power of Joy. May it reflect the love and light of God. And may your journey inspire others to find and fixate on their own Joy.

Thank you for allowing me to share this journey with you. I pray that your pursuit of Joy leads you to the fullness of God's promises, where Joy is not just a fleeting emotion but a sustainable and transformative way of being.

> *"May the God of hope fill you with all Joy and peace as you trust in Him, so that you may overflow with hope by the power of the Holy Spirit."*
>
> (Romans 15:13)

Go forth and live in Joy. The journey is yours; the Joy is yours, and the destination is worth it.

COACHING
YOURSELF
ON
JOY

JOY AMBASSADORS FROM THE BIBLE

1. King David

King David, a central figure in the Old Testament, was the second king of Israel and is described as a "man after God's own heart" (1 Samuel 13:14). He was a shepherd, warrior, poet, and musician who wrote many of the Psalms, which express a profound range of human emotion from despair and repentance to overwhelming Joy and praise. Despite his flaws and sins, such as his actions involving Bathsheba, David repeatedly turned back to God, displaying deep faith and repentance. His Joy and trust in God are evident in verses like Psalm 23 and Psalm 28:7, where he exults in God as his protector and deliverer.

2. Apostle Paul

Paul, originally Saul of Tarsus, was a Pharisee who persecuted early Christians before his dramatic conversion on the road to Damascus (Acts 9). After this encounter with the risen Christ, Paul became one of the New Testament's most prolific writers and missionaries. Despite enduring imprisonment, shipwrecks, beatings, and other trials, Paul radiated Joy, grounded in his unshakeable faith in Christ. His letters, like Philippians written from prison, emphasize rejoicing in the Lord always (Philippians 4:4). Paul's life exemplifies how Joy transcends circumstances when it is rooted in a relationship with God.

3. Mary, the mother of Jesus

Mary, a humble young woman from Nazareth, was chosen by God as the mother of Jesus Christ. Her faith and obedience are evident when the angel Gabriel announces she will conceive the Son of God (Luke 1:26-38). Mary's Joy in fulfilling God's plan is beautifully captured in the Magnificat (Luke 1:46-55), a song of praise expressing her gratitude for God's faithfulness and mercy. Mary's role extended beyond Jesus' birth. She was present at His first miracle and crucifixion, faithfully standing by Him throughout His life and ministry.

4. Mary Magdalene

Mary Magdalene was a devoted follower of Jesus, healed by Him from seven demons (Luke 8:2). She became one of His closest disciples and supported His ministry financially. Mary Magdalene's Joy is most powerfully displayed at the resurrection when she is the first to encounter the risen Christ (John 20:11-18). Her exclamation, "I have seen the Lord," marks her as the first witness of the Resurrection and an evangelist to the disciples. Mary's life exemplifies redemption, unwavering devotion, and the transformative Joy of encountering Jesus.

5. Anna the Prophetess

Anna was a devout widow and prophetess who worshiped in the temple day and night, fasting and praying (Luke 2:36-37). She encountered the infant Jesus when His parents brought Him to the temple, immediately recognizing Him as the long-awaited Messiah. Her Joy overflowed as she thanked God and spoke about Jesus to all who were waiting for the redemption of Israel (Luke 2:38). Anna's story highlights the Joy that comes from faithful devotion and the fulfillment of God's promises.

6. The Samaritan Woman at the Well

The Samaritan woman at the well is pivotal in the Gospel of John (John 4:1-42). An outcast due to her ethnicity and personal history, she encounters Jesus, who speaks to her with compassion and reveals Himself as the Messiah. Her transformation is immediate. She leaves her water jar and runs to tell her community about Jesus, inviting them to meet the One who *"told [her] everything [she] ever did."* Her Joy and testimony led many in her town to believe in Jesus, showcasing how an encounter with Him brings redemption and purpose.

COACHING
YOURSELF
ON
JOY

JOY AMBASSADORS TODAY

1. **Barbara A. Perkins**

    (Please see About the Author on page 143.)

2. **Iyanla Vanzant**

Iyanla Vanzant, a renowned spiritual teacher, life coach, and author, is known for her transformative work in helping people heal and find inner peace. Her show, *Iyanla: Fix My Life*, and numerous books, including *Acts of Faith*, reflect her profound wisdom and commitment to guiding others toward self-awareness and Joy. Iyanla's teachings emphasize forgiveness, authenticity, and embracing life's lessons as opportunities for growth. Her radiant personality and ability to connect deeply with others make her a beacon of Joy and inspiration for those seeking healing and fulfillment.

3. **Priscilla Shirer**

Priscilla Shirer is a gifted Bible teacher, author, and speaker known for her dynamic preaching and commitment to empowering others to deepen their faith. As the daughter of renowned pastor Tony Evans, Priscilla has made a name for herself through her ministry, books, and appearances in films like *War Room.* Her Joy is rooted in her passion for the Word of God and her ability to inspire others to live victoriously through faith. Through her ministry, Going Beyond, Priscilla helps individuals discover the power of a personal relationship with Christ.

4. Dr. Jacqueline "Jackie" McCullough

Dr. Jackie McCullough is a renowned preacher, pastor, and gospel artist whose ministry is marked by its Joy and passion for the Gospel. She founded The International Gathering at Beth Rapha, a church in New York, and is known for her powerful, spirit-filled sermons. Dr. McCullough's Joy stems from her unwavering faith in God and her commitment to teaching others about the transformative power of the Word. Her ministry is a beacon of hope and Joy, particularly for women seeking spiritual empowerment.

5. Dr. Cynthia L. Hale

Dr. Cynthia L. Hale is the founding and senior pastor of Ray of Hope Christian Church in Decatur, Georgia. She is a visionary leader and an inspiring preacher whose ministry is rooted in Joy, empowerment, and faith. Known for her powerful preaching style and ability to connect deeply with her congregation, Dr. Hale has been a trailblazer in ministry for African American women. Her Joy is evident in her dedication to uplifting others and her belief in the power of God to transform lives.

6.   Oprah Winfrey

Oprah Winfrey, a media mogul and philanthropist, is known for her vibrant personality and commitment to uplifting others. Despite a challenging childhood marked by poverty and trauma, Oprah has risen to become one of the most influential women in the world. Her Joy is deeply rooted in her faith and spiritual practices, which she openly shares through her shows, books, and public speaking. Oprah's ability to find Joy in personal growth, gratitude, and helping others live their best lives is evident in her inspiring words and actions.

7.   Michelle Obama

Michelle Obama, the former First Lady of the United States, is celebrated for her advocacy and accomplishments, and her warmth and Joy. Her sense of humor, candid reflections, and genuine connection with people have endeared her to millions. Michelle shares her journey of balancing challenges with gratitude and purpose in her memoir Becoming. She often emphasizes the importance of finding Joy in everyday moments and cultivating a life grounded in love, family, and service.

8.   Kamala Harris

Kamala Harris, the United States' 49th Vice President, embodies Joy and resilience as a trailblazing leader. As the first woman, first Black woman, and first South Asian woman to hold the office of Vice President, she has broken barriers with grace and determination.

Kamala's Joy is evident in her infectious laugh, optimism, and commitment to justice and equity. Her work as a public servant reflects her deep care for uplifting communities and inspiring future generations. Kamala's ability to face challenges with courage and Joy reminds us that even in demanding leadership roles, Joy can be a source of strength.

These African American women leaders, preachers, and ministers of the Gospel embody faith and ministry, inspiring countless others to embrace the Joy of the Lord in their own lives. They are powerful examples of how Joy can be lived and shared.

ABOUT THE AUTHOR

Barbara A. Perkins is an esteemed Executive Leadership Coach, author, and inspirational speaker dedicated to empowering individuals to achieve personal and professional growth. With over 25 years of experience in human and organizational development, Barbara has cultivated a unique approach to coaching that blends wisdom, compassion, and actionable strategies.

As the founder of Image Builders Etcetera, a leadership development and coaching firm, and Barbara A. Perkins Consultancy, LLC, she has worked with clients across various industries, guiding them to unlock their potential and foster high-performance teams. Barbara is committed to excellence and elevating those she is engaged. Through coaching and being on faculty at the Dorothy I. Height Global Leadership Academy, she desires to fill the pipeline with Black women ready to lead at home in the US and abroad.

An accomplished author of seven books on coaching, mentoring, and leadership, Barbara uses her writing to share insights and strategies that inspire others. Her deep faith and belief in the transformative power of Joy underpins her coaching philosophy, encouraging clients to embrace their journeys with hope and purpose. When not coaching or writing, Barbara enjoys time with her family: her husband, Stanley, two adult children, and a six-year-old grandson.

OTHERS BOOKS
BY AUTHOR
BARBARA A. PERKINS

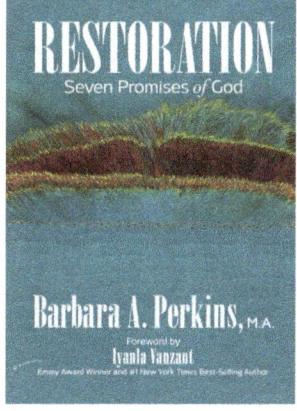

www.ingramcontent.com/pod-product-compliance
Lightning Source LLC
Chambersburg PA
CBHW051159120626
46547CB00012B/1128